Hey Addiction, Thanks for NOTHING

A Brutally Honest Guide to
Loving an Addict Without
Losing Your Mind

§

A Resource for All Humans that Love an Addict, including Therapists, Physicians, and Other Professionals

MEREDITH BEARDMORE
MA, LMHC

Published by:
LIBRARY TALES PUBLISHING
www.LibraryTalesPublishing.com
www.Facebook.com/LibraryTalesPublishing

Published in New York, New York.

For general information on our other products and services, please contact our Customer Care Department at 1-800-754-5016, or fax 917-463-0892.

978-1-956769-38-8
978-1-956769-39-5

TABLE OF CONTENTS

Author Background

Meredith Beardmore is a psychotherapist with a private practice just outside NYC, but you may know her as "Mend with Mere," which is the title of her successful YouTube Channel. She graduated from The Ohio State University with her master's degree in Clinical Mental Health Counseling, ranked #1 among the top ten programs in the nation by U.S. News & World Report. She specializes in substance abuse – supporting family members of addicted populations and treating emerging adults with various concerns, from identity development to depression. Meredith utilizes therapeutic modalities such as Acceptance and Commitment Therapy (ACT), Cognitive Behavioral Therapy (CBT), and Client-Centered approaches, and incorporates Mindfulness and Expressive Arts Techniques into her work. Meredith is the former AOD (Alcohol and Other Drugs) Coordinator at Iona College, a member of the Association of Contextual Behavioral Sciences (ACBS), the American Counseling Association, and a Certified Suicide Prevention Gatekeeper. She is also an Educator/Facilitator, training other clinicians on substance use and client suicide for attendees to obtain CEUs (Continuing Education Credits) to renew their professional license to practice in N.Y. State. In addition, she has presented at various conferences on using Expressive Arts Techniques in Group Counseling.

Meredith created her popular YouTube Channel, "Mend with Mere," to reach a larger audience since private practice began feeling limiting. Meredith initially set out to provide discussion around topics usually saved for therapy; however, she quickly began reacting and dissecting the lyrics of musical artists, mainly Taylor Swift, after a subscriber requested it. This "glitch" has led to thousands of subscribers, garnering over 2 million views and more than 100,000 hours of watch time. Viewers eagerly tune in for Meredith's reactions, guidance, and support. Aside from her online presence, Meredith is a public speaker, often hired for speaking engagements and training sessions. She has also contributed to ***The Huffington Post*** and ***BuzzFeed***, and has been published in Colman McCarthy's "Teaching Peace."

Having loved several people with addiction issues from her teens onwards, Meredith has been writing and drawing about these experiences for a long time. Now, she brings her personal and professional knowledge about the absurdity of these situations, along with her Expressive Arts Techniques and sense of humor, to those who, like her, love someone with addiction issues. Meredith lives with her Mini Aussie dog, Reese, and her son, Jules, in New Rochelle, NY.

Foreword

To the readers of this book – Yes, my sister shares some things about me…and while I don't enjoy revisiting the past, she has my consent to share her experience of my addiction. While we don't always agree, we definitely are on the same page about two things – the need for more healing around addiction and laughing about fucked-up shit. Love you, Mere!

Leslie Beardmore-Hibbitts

Dedication

This book is dedicated to my grandpa and Jules. Grandpa - Thank you for encouraging me to write from beyond the grave. Jules - Thank you for choosing me as your mother.

Hey Addiction,
thanks for
NOTHING

INTRODUCTION
The Overwhelm

So, you picked up my book—welcome! I'm happy (or not so happy) to have you here. Despite the eye-catching title, you might be wondering what this book is all about. Is it serious? Funny? Absurd? Yes, yes, and yes. Most importantly, though, it's a safe space for anyone who has supported a loved one through addiction, from someone who's been there.

I'm Meredith Beardmore, a veteran psychotherapist who specializes in supporting loved ones affected by substance abuse. While scary to admit, I, too, have loved ones whose addiction permeated into every facet of their existence, and I've lived in the shadows of its harm. I wish that being an expert in this field would mean that I could "save" my loved ones from their disease and that

I'd be exempt from suffering peripherally. But alas, addiction does not discriminate; it does not care about your gender, socioeconomic status, or job title. It is universal. One cannot escape being ensnared in the collateral damage of it all.

For a long time, I did not want to disclose that I too was suffering much like my patients. Even for me, as a woman in a position of perceived power, I was scared to be transparent with my experiences and pain. I knew the stigma my patients spoke of and felt its stifling control. However, I knew full well the power of vulnerability, often encouraging my clients to move past the fear and speak their truth, so how could I not do the same? Vulnerability feels exposing, yet, I have only seen positive effects from being transparent about who I am and what I've gone through. Also, who really wants to sit across from a therapist that hasn't been through some shit? Not me.

So, the veneer of professionalism will be left behind so that honesty, inclusivity, and especially realness can prevail. Realness means that profanity will be welcomed since I will no longer filter myself to make the brutality of addiction more digestible. It isn't fucking digestible; it feels like you are choking on your own vomit, and there's no one to turn you on your side. There is no book on the market that provides a momentary respite from the dark cloud of addiction, and this quite frankly pissed me off. Therefore, I have created a place of solace for people seeking a refuge from what I call "The Overwhelm" of loving someone experiencing addiction (more on that later). Do you need this safe space where you can come, flaws and all? Think about the following statements and make a mental note if you relate.

You suspect someone you love has an addiction.

If you've felt even a mild pang of curiosity about it, chances are they probably do have an addiction. They might be adept at hiding it, or deep down, you might not want to see it.

You love someone with an addiction, and you want to save them.

You are heartbroken by their agony and feel helpless. Wanting to protect this person, you keep their secret quiet. Some people in your life have noticed a subtle change in you. But you're putting on a brave face, believing that everything will be over soon, and that you'll be able to save them.

You love someone with an addiction, and you feel confused.

You keep trying to anticipate their needs and reactions, stepping in when you can to help them avoid further consequences, but they are not stopping. While you are getting really good at maneuvering around their volatility, you cannot steady the waters like you used to. You go in and out of questioning your own sanity and spend hours completely ridden with anxiety or crying your eyes out.

You love someone with an addiction and damn it, they are going to change if it's the last thing you do!

It doesn't matter if you have to scream, plead, cry, or act like a total fucking maniac; they will quit this addiction! You no longer care about who knows; you are going to make sure they take this as seriously as you do! So, it has to stop NOW! I mean, what the actual FUCK!

You love someone with an addiction, and you are defeated.

You feel emotionally destroyed, are beaten up by the pain, and are waving the white flag of surrender. You realize it is beyond your control, wonder how you got here, and are shocked by who you have become. You need help because your heart is now breaking again, but this time, it is breaking for *you*.

If these resonate with you in some way, I'm so sorry. Please know you are not alone; there are many of us. And if you have no idea what I'm talking about, feel fucking lucky.

Ask Me Anything with Myself

Answers I Wish I Had Before Starting This Journey

Have you ever dealt with a loved one with addiction issues?

Yes, I was lucky enough to experience that chaos very early on. My sister dealt with heroin addiction while I was still in high school. I handled this by trying to distract my parents by being a perfectionist overachiever, which led to resentment, disappointment, and ultimately hating my life and myself. I desperately needed help understanding this addiction, but since we were all new to this, I took her addiction on like a warrior. I felt I could make an impact and got my heart broken in the process several times. Therapy continues to help; I love her very much, and we are super close now. Time and boundaries did the trick, and I no longer took her addiction personally, neither believing I caused it nor thinking I could cure it. I came to understand that I am only responsible for my own life. But, again, that was just the beginning. I have had to "unlearn" many behaviors I learned from this time.

You are or were in therapy? But you are also a therapist?

Yes, it is good practice for all therapists to continue to engage in their own personal therapy, as it makes us better therapists. I work with families affected by addiction, people struggling with addiction concerns, and clients experiencing issues like anxiety, depression, body image, and identity development. I have witnessed the profound impact of therapy. Even though it can evoke my personal emotions or memories, I know the power of sitting with someone who truly "gets" the effects of addiction.

Who inspired this book?

That is very complex. Myself, my family, my husband, my friends, and my clients.

So, you just started drawing fucked up scenes resulting from addiction?!

Yea, kind of. I am often asked for book recommendations. Clients want support, understanding, and most importantly, humor to cope with the insanity of loving an addict. I could not find one. I began drawing some of the ridiculous scenarios based on both the stories clients shared with me and experiences from my own life. During one session, I presented a drawing that depicted the exact scenario my client was experiencing. We laughed together for a good five minutes. It was therapeutic. The depicted insanity provided a much-needed comic relief. The drawing and processing of the picture helped to identify the exact behaviors the client was making in response to the addict that they needed to stop. I'm not sure how many additional sessions would've been needed for that client to make the connection. Still, I can guarantee you that when art imitates life, it deeply resonates. It cuts through defense mechanisms, allowing individuals to clearly see the necessary changes in their behavior, just as addicts do.

"You alluded to other experiences with addiction and "unlearning" behaviors. Can you elaborate?

My marriage has weathered the storm of addiction, but unfortunately, even while specializing in addiction, I became the classic enabler with all the hallmark features, such as denial and anger, a splash of savior complex, and a hefty dose of codependency (more on that later)."

Therapists can be skilled in working with others but may still miss, distract from, or ignore the obvious issues in their own lives (anyone telling you otherwise is lying, unaware, or full of shit). Addiction is a disease that affects the entire family and acts as a breeding ground for codependency. If you're unfamiliar with codependency, it's when you feel pretty much worthless if you are not needed. Why is codependency so prevalent in families with addiction? The answer is shame. Shame and codependency are closely linked. The individual struggling with addiction is undoubtedly suffering, with shame deeply intertwined in the development of the addiction. The people surrounding the addict can fall into a cycle of "fixing."

Adults in healthy relationships are able to speak for themselves, set boundaries, and recognize their own limits. When someone, like myself, is raised in a home lacking these traits and where addiction is present, they begin to see and understand that relationships can often be imbalanced. Over time, this imbalance becomes normalized.

For instance, I witnessed my parents obsessively try to "fix" my sister's addiction. When we couldn't reach her, the whole family experienced heightened anxiety. Keep in mind—cellphones were just becoming commonly used at this time. That's right—no location sharing, "Find My Friends" app, NOTHING. When my sister was in trouble, we went to great lengths to prevent her from facing the consequences of her actions. We believed we were genuinely helping her, not understanding that we were perpetuating secrecy and control. I felt my role was to distract my parents from their pain by excelling in school, sports, or any other activity. I believed that I was proving to them that they were still great parents, especially since they expressed feelings of failure. However, when my achievements didn't provide lasting distraction or happiness, I questioned my worth. I feel an urge now to defend my parents and minimize my own experience, but the truth is they were doing their best amidst the worst of circumstances—plunging into the depths of despair—and it was problematic all the same.

Okay, I'll get back to my marriage story. Due to my sister's addiction, I unknowingly became codependent. Before I truly understood how the disease affected me, with its unhealthy coping mechanisms, or contributed to my low self-esteem (feeling worthy only if others approved of me), I unconsciously sought out people who needed me. That was familiar, and it made me feel valuable. As humans, we gravitate towards familiar people and situations. Have you ever wondered why you often end up in friendships or relationships, with people who have attributes reminiscent of one or both of your parents? I'm not talking about Freud's potentially contentious theory (sorry, my psychoanalytic friends) that kids are attracted to the opposite-sex parent, which he called the Oedipus complex. I'm referring to imprinting, the theory proposed by psychologist and researcher John Gottman. His theory suggests that we are psychologically conditioned to be attracted to a distinct parental personality type by 18 months old. This "imprinting" arises from factors, including, perhaps most importantly, how we received (or were deprived of) love, intimacy, and security from our parent(s) or caregivers.

I think it's a mix of imprinting and attachment styles. The works of Bartholomew and Horowitz discussed the four different attachment styles and how our psychological and social conditioning forms these attachment patterns, thus becoming our subconscious blueprint for relationship or friend attraction and selection. This is not always negative, as one's imprinting and formative attachment styles often present a combination of desirable and challenging traits. This became clear when discussing my issues with my friend Kate, who also happens to be a badass clinical psychologist. She said, "Mere, I'm hearing some attachment stuff going on…like anxious avoidant…" Shit. How did I not see that? When I mentioned even therapists have blind spots when it comes to themselves, I truly meant it.

Admittedly, I veered off-topic to reach my main point: both you and I can recognize and accept our patterns and roles in the addiction cycle once we understand their origins—Yay for therapy! This recognition isn't about placing blame but rather about understanding these patterns and considering change. While it's true that addicts can sometimes act irrationally or impulsively, we must acknowledge our active role in responding to and sometimes enabling these behaviors. Of course, there are exceptions, but most often, we aren't simply passive observers. The addict doesn't force us into any of the batshit crazy situations we might find ourselves in. If anyone said this to me when I was younger, I would have debated them until I was blue in the face or imagined ways in which I could physically harm them for not "understanding" my reality. But with clarity comes the realization: our reactions to triggering situations either help or harm us, and we have control over those reactions.

Once you can see yourself clearly, you can notice how your behavior and response to certain provoking situations either *benefits* or *hurts* you, and that you have control over your response.

I'll give an example from my own life. I received a phone call informing me that my husband had crashed his car into a light pole, and he asked me to pick him up from the scene. Before, I would have jumped in the car and raced there like a savior, the one to "make it all better." Then, I'd find myself in a rage once all the information about the event settled in. My rage would probably worsen further if he did not give me the acknowledgment I thought I deserved for "helping" him (good old resentment and codependency). This behavior would showcase a less than beautiful side of myself where I'd lash out and accuse him of ruining everything. No, no one can genuinely ruin everything. But I had a part in it.

In the past, I would never have stopped to think about how I felt about what was being asked of me; I would have said yes instinctively. This instinct goes back to what was modeled for me in my family, their core beliefs that "blood is thicker than water" and "if a family member needs you,

you drop everything." (Sorry, mom and dad, but no, no, you don't.) It relates to how I respond to being needed, as if it signifies my value. This feeling is deeply tied to my sense of worthiness. Now, I know I am enough. That sounds so cliché, and I cringe writing it, but it's the fucking truth. No one can tell you if you're good enough. Only *you* can, and it isn't fair to make someone else responsible for making you feel that way.

So, how did I respond to that phone call? I said no. That's it. No. "No, I will not come and pick you up." It was simple, but it felt anything but that when I first thought of my own needs. I still had to call Kate to make sure I was making the right decision because it didn't feel right in my body. In my body, I felt as though I was betraying my values and was sick to my stomach. However, my mind knew that I had a choice, and that I was a separate being (Yes, I realize that saying "a separate being" sounds strange.) Still, I mean that when you're trapped in the cycle of addiction and codependency, you focus more on the needs, moods, and desires of others than on your own. You might deny your own needs for the sake of others, which can look and feel like enabling and people-pleasing. You may even struggle to identify your own feelings and look to others for validation. You might possess an exaggerated sense of responsibility for the actions of others. Sometimes, your mood is dictated by someone else because you can't feel happy if they aren't. It can become so overwhelming that you lose touch with your baseline mood.

Taking care of others seems easier than taking control of yourself; thus, saying "no" isn't easy. It *feels* like a violation. I often repeat, "saying no is saying yes to myself." I think Oprah once said that. Bow to the Queen - I adore her. And it's a reminder that helps immensely. I have to convince myself that having boundaries is okay. If this resonates with you, understand that it can become easier.

When I set boundaries, I make the other person deal with their consequences. See, I was never truly helping my sister, partner, or friends by "saving" them from their consequences. If anything, I kept them from hitting rock bottom faster and facing the reality of their addiction issues. So, saying 'no' not only means saying 'yes' to myself but also represents an act of love. If you truly love someone, you can lovingly detach and state, "I love you so much, and because of that, I cannot save you, but I'm here for you when you are ready to get better."

You are telling me that you don't have to do anything?

No, not until the person is ready. Sometimes, the actions that would help them can seem hurtful and cruel if applied to non-addicts. Unfortunately, even the best ways to respond to an addict can overwhelm those who love them, drowning them in guilt, grief, doubt, and rage.

What if people tell you that you are being cruel by not helping more? What about the people that give advice or suggestions?

Fuck them... or if you need a kinder response, I defer to this quote: "Unless someone has been in battle armor beside you, fighting the fight being brought to their knees, with their heart broken and their resilience tested, it's not for them to judge." – Karen Young"

I think I get it now. So I focus on myself and wait til they are ready?

Yes.

But what if they're never ready?

This question makes me feel sad because the truth is, some people are never ready, and the only choice you have then is to let go. Letting go doesn't mean you stop loving them - it never means that. You can still tell them you'll be there when they're ready to change. This will lovingly put the responsibility for their healing in their hands and hear me clearly when I say this, that is the only place it should be.

Damn. No further questions.

§

Defining My Terms

As discussed, the veneer of professionalism is being lifted for realness and for the sake of brevity. Although I do not want to label my loved ones as "addicts," it is easier than repeating "a loved one experiencing substance use concerns." When I refer to someone as an "addict" throughout this book, please consider it as an umbrella term that encompasses many addictions – gambling, spending, eating, substances, etc.

Addiction is a chronic disease that, unfortunately, is riddled with stigma. There are inaccurate beliefs that an addict has had some "moral failing" and that they therefore cannot recover on their own. Since labels can be limiting, I aim to speak in a relatable way, avoiding clinical terms, and not contribute to those stigmas. Terms like "junkie" and "druggie" are hurtful to me, and if I ever hear them from your mouth, know that they will not be met with warmth. Consider this a fair warning. Please know these negative slang words are in no way connected to *my* term "addict." I never use this term derogatorily.

Take a Moment with Me

Alright, dear readers, I am prepared for a big skeptical eye roll from you here. But I've included some reflection and meditation questions, as well as exercises, at the end of each chapter. I know what you're thinking: who wants to do something that feels like a school activity? Me neither, but I promise it'll be worth it. Consider it akin to physical exercise: challenging in the moment yet fulfilling afterward (just think of all benefits!) These reflection sections serve a similar purpose.

See, I may not have all the answers, having not walked in your shoes, but I aim to guide you in discovering your own answers through these reflections. Since you've probably had to do a lot of things you really don't want to be doing, I totally support you if you choose to skip that part. So, no pressure. Sound good?

CHAPTER ONE
Excuse me; I'm the Crazy One?

You Down with OPP (Other People's Problems)?

Everything in my family was so woven together that I was unsure where I began and my mother ended. I thought that was how every family must be, but I now recognize that my parents should have shielded me from my sister's addiction. I didn't need to know every detail, and my inability to improve the situation created a rage inside me that led to the infamous "Day of the Toaster."

Day of the Toaster

It was a warm late spring morning back in 2002. After my mom and I got some snacks, we headed to my sister's apartment. Our weekly ritual was to sit in the back right parking spot and spy on her. This parking spot was shaded by a tree hanging down, camouflaging our faces as we speculated about who the people coming in and out were. My mom seemed more anxious than usual and began spiraling. She worried that my sister would be kicked out, arrested, lose custody of her kids, die from an overdose, or hurt someone under the influence. Then my mom would discuss how she didn't understand where she went wrong, why God would inflict our family with this disease, and how she thought her girls would grow up to live down the street from her and lead a lovely, peaceful life where we'd raise our children together. My mom never could have imagined that her daughter could be an addict. My mother's eyebrows stayed furrowed, and her eyes crinkled, becoming watery.

I tried my best to remind my mother of all the good in our lives. I reminded her that she still had me and that I'd never put her through such pain. I tried to distract her by bringing up the recent A- I got on my Chemistry test and discussing my plans to run for student council next year. But that day, my words seemed to have no effect; she continued to stare off with tearful eyes. Unfortunately, when my mother cries, it tears me to pieces, and I want to destroy whatever is causing her pain. I despise this trait in myself. I learned it from my father, whose typical response to tears was anger - a response generated from his childhood trauma. He, too, felt powerless when watching his mother cry. Because of this, my mother would feel as if she had to keep it all hidden inside. I feel bad about that. However, on this day, destroying was all I wanted to do. I had enough.

I do not fully remember what I said before getting out of the car, but I slammed the door and started walking straight to the stairs. I banged on the apartment door with my fist until a random person opened it. I just pushed the door against them and began screaming, "Ok, everybody out!" A group of skanky-ass wannabe deadheads were nodding off on the couch, but some looked up. When no one got up, I started breaking and throwing things. The apartment building was three floors up, and at one point (so I'm told), I grabbed a toaster, stomped to the balcony, and chucked it off into the yard, smiling as it descended onto some muddy grass. I genuinely do not remember the rest of the day. There is no more memory that I can conjure up, but later on that day, the father of one of the skanks called my mom. He was so distraught that her "crazy daughter" had broken his daughter's toaster. "Wait, what? Excuse me? *I* am the 'crazy daughter'? WTF?" But he was kind of right; I lost it but was still stunned to be considered the "crazy" one."

In retrospect, I mostly stayed away from drugs and alcohol because my sister struggled with addiction. However, rather than turning to substances, I acted out in peculiar ways. For example, my best friend and I would go to lunch at Wendy's almost every day and order a large, sweet tea. Any sweet tea not consumed by the end of lunch would be used as a comedic weapon. We were once stuck in our car behind a man hauling his boat into his driveway. Impatient with the wait, we chucked the sweet tea out of our window, watching it explode upon hitting the inside of the boat, ice spraying everywhere like a hailstorm and tea splattering the interior. This gave us pure joy. (On behalf of Chelsie and me, we apologize to that man).

See, people can only handle so much stress before it comes out. While I was masking it all with smiles and good grades, I was sad and angry. I prayed to God that something would happen to stop the pain. In Buddhism, there's this saying that there are two things we can count on in life: change and suffering. At first, this frustrated me. Later, I felt relief. If change was inevitable, then I held onto the hope that perhaps the chaos caused by my sister's addiction would eventually end.

And yes, the change finally came when my sister's soon-to-be ex-husband crashed his motorcycle, breaking every bone in his face and almost dying. She got on a plane to be with him, and my parents and I found peace. It was the first time we could actually exhale because she was under someone else's care. Her ex-husband's mother, who is a nurse, helped my sister get on Methadone. Even though I am not a fan of my ex-brother-in-law, I am grateful for the choice he made that day to ride a motorcycle without a helmet.

But back to the "Day of the Toaster," I recently asked my sister about it from her perspective, and she said I was really scary. She thought that I had spearheaded the whole mission. While I basically had, it dawned on us that I was just 16 at the time. We sat there for a moment, taking in that fact. I have always acted like the older sibling, even though my sister is almost four years older than me. Still, I wasn't typically this kind of person, so something must have snapped in me. Looking back, I think I believed I had the power to change my sister, to save her and my family, but in truth I was powerless. I've been harsh on myself for not realizing this sooner, but no one taught me that. No one reassured me that I would get through this and that I needed to to put the focus back on myself. It should have been my parents' responsibility to guide me and protect me. However, there was still significant stigma around therapy at the time, and seeking help would mean admitting their daughter was an addict.

At that time, and even today, being considered an addict was akin to wearing a scarlet letter. All the cruel names, such as loser and junkie, would not only be associated with my sister but also, in my parents' eyes, with them. My parents lacked a reference point for what was unfolding; they were in survival mode. I hold immense compassion for them, as I can't even imagine having to endure such a situation as a parent. Yet, their obsessive focus on concealing and stopping her addiction was hurting me, even though they never intended to. They simply couldn't see the impact it had on me. I was inadvertently entangled in every facet of the ordeal. No one was protecting *me* from anything. Maybe I always seemed mature or "grown-up," but it wasn't my responsibility to shoulder.

Correction: Carol Beardmore has informed me that she did, in fact, protect me from many things that I am *still* not privy to. Thank you, Mom.

Deep in the Trenches

I am not a fan of war, nor do I like when people use war (or sports) metaphors. Ironically, I'm about to do so because trying to save someone from addiction truly feels like war. I'm not envisioning something like a nuclear war but something akin to WWI, where you just have a rifle and limited medical assistance for wounds. (They would often use a guillotine to amputate back then—WTF?) And you have to shit in a hole while simultaneously fighting for your life. When you willingly entered this war, determined to fight your loved one's addiction, you didn't realize you'd be in the trenches alone. But you are. With each dig into the ground, every sandbag stacked, and each duckboard mounted, you built this trench for yourself. You've created a home there. While you can barely eat or sleep, shivering and covered in mud, you continue to peer over the edge, assessing the right moment to attack the addiction. You are still oblivious to the fact that this war is not yours to fight. You are disillusioned, unaware that you are deep in the trenches of "The Overwhelm."

When I was unable to sleep one night, tired from scrolling through pop culture news, I finally decided to visit my nighttime friends, Thesaurus and Dictionary.com. Naturally, a feeling or event often pops into my mind. To relax, I explore the possible meanings and etiology of words that can encompass the complexity of that feeling or event (I blame this compulsion on the internet.) For example, I used to be slightly disappointed by my constant use of the term "The Overwhelm" to describe the state when you believe you're helping a loved one with an addiction, but you're actually interfering. I would encourage myself to find a better term. However, when I consulted my friends about the word "overwhelm," I let out an audible "ah yes, yes" upon confirming that "overwhelm" perfectly captured the sentiment.

This verb has many definitions, such as:

- To make helpless, as with greater force or deep emotion; crush; overpower.
- Have a strong emotional effect on.
- Give too much of a thing to someone; inundate.
- Bury or drown beneath a huge mass.
- Defeat completely.

This word started as a medieval sea term, meaning to capsize – to engulf, surge over, and submerge. When in "The Overwhelm," you don't think you will "drown beneath the mass" of it, but you will. You are still living in the delusion that the addiction will be defeated, but in reality, you have no power, no ability to fight someone else's addiction. Wait, you need visuals? Cool, that helps me too. Take a gander at some scenarios from my life, my friends, and my clients who capture "The Overwhelm."

Ever snuck into the basement with a ruler at 3 a.m. to pour out 1/4 of a bottle of liquor and refill it with the exact amount of water, so it won't be detected?

Remember, you are not Walter White.

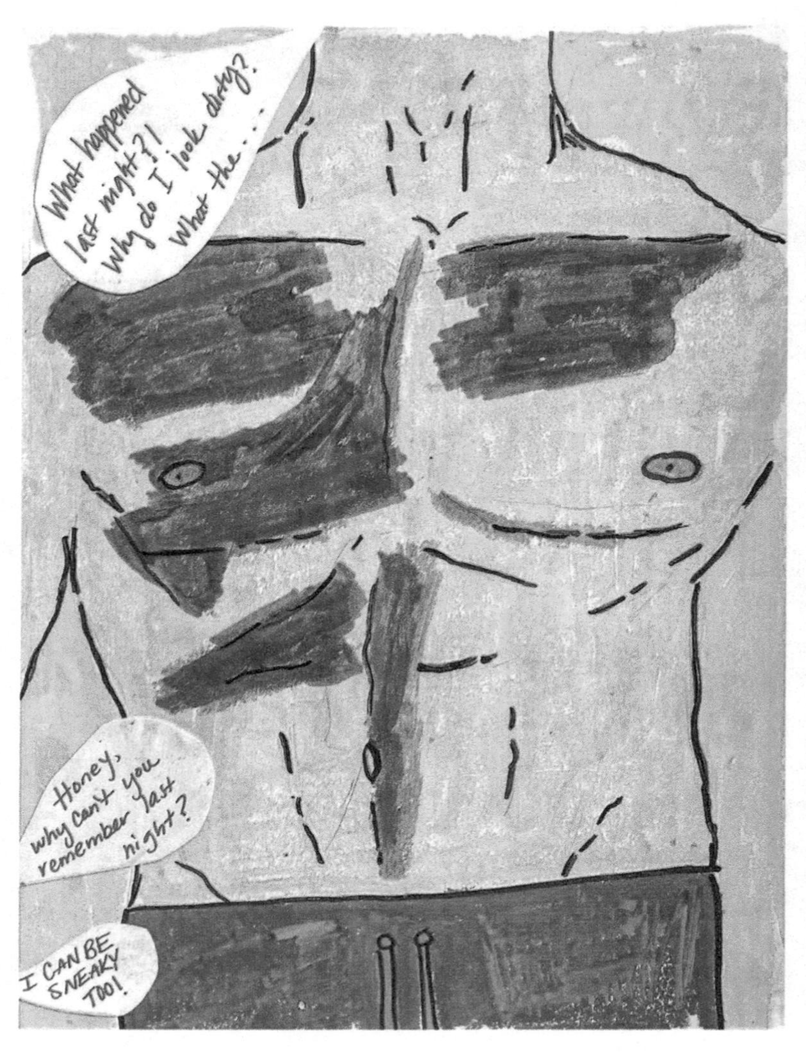

Ever been so angry that you gave sunless tanner instead of lotion to your intoxicated husband after he showered, so that he'd wake up looking dirty? You have? Cool, me too.

Anger comes out in the strangest ways.

Ever visualized a chessboard on the ceiling and gone through all the different moves the addict could make, so you could stealthily intervene?

You are not Beth Harmon from "The Queen's

Gambit"; she was hallucinating on pills.

Ever stolen your sister's car from her drug dealer's house, only to have the drug dealer show up at your door because you forgot to put your garage door down?

Ah, it's the small details that count.

Ever stayed up all night spying on them, only to regret your stalker status when you can barely function the next day?

Say it with me: "I CANNOT CHANGE THEM."

Ever contemplated letting your partner walk into the hotel hallway naked because they couldn't find the bathroom?

I know, I know – you didn't want them to experience the consequences of being blackout drunk before 12 p.m.

Ever hidden their car keys so they can't drive, but then forget where you hid them?

Sucks, especially when you need their help to search for them.

Whiskey dick anyone?
If you know, you know.

Consequences = Magic

You are taking on too much; you are inundated with pain and feeling defeated because this is <u>not</u> your fight. Stop for a moment—when has shielding someone from the consequences of their decisions ever been a good thing? Stepping in only messes up your own life. Yes, it can start so innocently, with the best intentions, but just like the illustrated scenarios—BAM! You are fucked.

You've heard the saying that people have to reach rock bottom before they can change, right? It's true, so won't you kindly step aside? You are actually being more harmful by not stepping aside. It is an act of love *to* step aside. You demonstrate love for a person by confirming your belief in their potential to change. You can support them when they're ready, but until then, it's best to step aside.

Ways to Step Aside: Answering to Myself

Let them wake up in their own urine. Let them walk down a hotel hallway naked. Let them get arrested. Let them sleep the whole day away and miss an important meeting. Let them face their own consequences. LET THEM.

Sorry, but that sounds really harsh.

Yes, it may *sound* harsh, but remember, this action is rooted in love.

Yeah, but you probably don't have kids, and when kids are involved, it's more complicated.

Wrong and wrong. It's not complicated; in fact, it's quite straightforward. I have a scrumptious little boy who makes my heart fill up in a way I never imagined it could, so I can tell you from experience: First, you must shield children from destructive behavior, neglect, and verbal or physical arguments. If this occurs, you must ensure that the children are safe and protected. This entails prioritizing your children's and your own well-being over the addict's concerns and any worries about what other people might think. Of course, you don't want the parent of your child to not be a part of your child's life, go to jail, or experience any adverse consequences of their choices. But you have to check with yourself why you are actually intervening.

For example, your loved one might end up in jail due to their addiction. Is your decision to intervene motivated by the desire to prevent them and the children from experiencing embarrassment? Or is your intervention inadvertently preventing your loved one from reaching a point where they *decide* to make a change? You should be more focused, always, on the latter because consequences are magic. Truly, they make change happen faster than you could ever imagine.

When I met my husband, he seemed to be clean-cut; he didn't drink alcohol. But since I love a bad boy, he would often partake in using cannabis. His negative feelings about drinking were firm. Long before weed became recreationally legal in New York, he openly criticized the regressive nature of alcohol being legal while marijuana was not. He would discuss how people typically don't drive when they smoke weed, feeling more relaxed and sedated, and how there's no hangover the next day. He also emphasized that you don't become more aggressive when high, and he pointed out that alcohol is much more dangerous and addictive. While these points could be made about alcohol without comparing it to weed, his conviction was attractive to me, especially since my Aunt Kristy died on her 17th birthday due to a drunk driver.

Fast forward eight years later, my husband and I are engaged with a 2-year-old boy during the first pandemic since 1918. He's out of work for 7 months, and I'm working more than ever, supporting my patients through an unpredictable time. Innocently enough, my husband tried a mixed drink after watching my silly side blossom following my enjoyment of some gin. During that time, I was constantly stressed and somber, so we welcomed the change. We needed a reprieve from the uncertainty of the pandemic. Unfortunately, the drinking crept up on him and us, and two years later, I asked him for a separation.

What happened in those two years?!

It feels like both a blur and a nightmare. My husband's addiction had gotten so bad - SO BAD. I can have a drink or two and then be done. Alcohol upsets my stomach, and I'm convinced it contributes to UTIs (excuse the TMI). These are primarily the reasons I avoid it. Yet, it became my husband's primary means of stress relief, and he undoubtedly had stress.

My husband has an incredible work ethic, and his career gave him - like most people - a purpose. So when the pandemic took his career away, he was in a dark place. This was compounded by my growing suspicion that our son was on the spectrum. Many people, especially men, have difficulty facing the fact that their child may have some "struggles" they did not anticipate.

After one of many evaluations, a speech pathologist met with both my husband and me. She reviewed the behaviors she had noted that aligned with symptoms of autism. Many of the behaviors mentioned were ones that my husband could identify with. As my husband slowly recognized that he might be on the spectrum himself, he felt a deep sense of guilt and shame, as if he were "defective" in some way. Unfortunately, he did not share his thoughts and feelings about this for a long time. Once work started back up, the drinking worsened progressively.

So, *where are these so-called "consequences" that equal magic?*

I'm about to get to that. We began to argue. I started enabling him, then resented him for "making me" do so, and he transformed into someone else. The charismatic, gentle, hilarious, and kind human I had chosen to create a life and child with was gone. I would see quick little glimpses of him – just enough to make me believe that this was no big deal and that it would all go away soon. But it didn't. Soon, I was gone too; I became someone else.

Then who were you?

I was the worst version of myself. I was angry and sad most of the time. I had dealt with depression and anxiety on and off throughout my life, but *this* was different. This was a deep pain, a grief so vast, and a profound mourning for what could have been. There were days I would cry and cry, hiding in the bathroom or stepping outside so my son wouldn't hear me. I'd become so angry with him, but I was really angry with myself because I couldn't stop or fix it. No amount of pleading, screaming, or crying would make him understand how bad it had gotten. One night, when he was getting out of the shower intoxicated and asked me to hand him the lotion, I gave him sunless tanner, but he didn't notice. I'm translucent (often called Casper by the boys in middle school), so I keep sunless tanner on hand just to look alive. Much to my sick delight, my husband woke up looking really dirty. REALLY dirty. I asked him what happened and played dumb. I got this surly enjoyment out of the fact that I did this and had some kind of control. This sounds relatively "harmless," but it worsened; we began spewing venom toward each other daily.

I finally convinced him to go to treatment, and he relented. However, when the time came, he could not bring himself to do it. So, I packed up, went to my friend's house, and asked for a separation. I couldn't do it anymore. I said our son deserves at least one healthy parent, and his addiction was making me unhealthy and ugly. I was ashamed of how I was treating him and, ultimately, myself in response to his addiction. I explained that his addiction was overshadowing the love and attention our son needed, and that I couldn't let his addiction continue to pull me down. I couldn't stay in a marriage like this. I said he may not understand why I'm doing this right now, but I believe this is not who he wants to be and that he can change. Asking my husband for a separation was the most excruciating decision.

How'd he react?

He went to treatment the next day.

Damn. That must have felt like magic.

Not at the time. I was honestly surprised that he went to treatment. I also got angry because I wished I had done this sooner if I knew it would affect him.

Sounds like you had many reasons to do that sooner.

Yes, I did, but I thought I could 'save' him. I am a therapist, after all! I expected too much of myself, thought too highly of my abilities, didn't admit my limitations, and didn't practice what I preach. I was selfish in believing I could handle it all, especially since I wanted to avoid what I feared the most: breaking up my family. But ultimately, avoiding making that ultimatum kept the magic from happening. The consequence of losing me "magically" made him see the light.

So it's all better now?

I don't believe there will ever be a time when everything is 'all better.' We all bring our own baggage into relationships, and it's our responsibility to be aware of it and do our best to *not* aggravate each other's trauma.

Reflection Time

Take a moment to sit quietly and think about your family. Have you ever felt as if you were "woven together" with another family member, or several?

____

If so, did this occur before, during, or after your loved one's addiction? Don't judge any feelings or thoughts that come up; simply bring awareness to them.

Have you ever acted out in a way that was incongruent with who you are or want to be? (For example, sending a random toaster flying, as I did)

Have you ever experienced intense anger in response to someone's addiction? If not, which other emotions have come up for you?

____

____

____

____

____

____

Sometimes people visualize emotions as colors[1]. If you already do this, awesome; if not, let's try it out. Take a moment to think about the colors that may be evoked within you in response to your loved one's addiction and scribble, draw, or pound the crayon until it breaks in the space below:

____

____

____

____

____

____

____

____

____

____

____

____

____

____

____

____

1. This is called synesthesia; it's a neurological condition where information that is meant to stimulate one of your senses, but instead stimulates others as well. Fun fact: Nikola Tesla, Beyoncé, and Pharrell are some famous people who have this condition.

I used a war analogy and the term "The Overwhelm" to describe the state in which you still believe you can help the addict but are getting crushed in the process. What term or phrase would you use to describe this experience?

What is coming up for you when you view these scenarios?

Do you connect with any of these scenarios?

What scenarios have you encountered that weren't depicted above? Have some fun reflecting on those moments—I promise, it's a good time. Laughing about the situations I've found myself in always helps, and I hope you can do the same. If you're artistic, consider drawing those scenes in the space below. If you find the process therapeutic, get a sketchbook. Dedicate it to your version of "The Overwhelm." Embrace your youthful, playful side: order crayons, colored pencils, or even paint. Or, if you prefer, cut out images from magazines and paste them in. Remember, there are no rules here. Let your creativity run wild!

Have you ever stopped the addict from facing their consequences? Be real with yourself here. Sometimes, we might not be aware that we are doing this, so closely examine your reactions or behaviors that may have interfered with their consequences.

____

____

____

____

____

____

How did you feel afterward? You may have interfered many times (no judgment, I have too). Examine what you felt during the different times. Did your feelings change over time?

____

____

____

____

____

____

Now, think about when you have set boundaries with the addict and allowed them to be responsible for their consequences. Was this difficult to do? Easy? Somewhere in between? What emotions came up for you?

____

____

____

____

____

____

____

____

How do you feel after reading that stepping aside is an act of love?

____

____

____

____

____

____

When I'm struggling to step aside, I will repeatedly recite affirmations until I feel a sense of calm. Take a look at the affirmations below:

§

Step Aside Affirmations

It is an act of love to step aside.

This is not your battle. Step aside.

You show love by believing in their ability to change. Step aside.

You will support them when they are ready to change. Step aside.

CHAPTER TWO
Knife In My Chest

Insurmountable Grief

In my life, I have experienced the death of loved ones. I have grieved, but somehow, this grief was different.

While discussing the loss with my close friends, I couldn't articulate my grief. My friends validated this experience in a whole new way.

"This grief is complicated and different than anything else," said Kate. "Look, the soul of the person you loved is no longer in that body."

Damn.

"You are holding a boundary with a body that the person you loved used to inhabit."

That's it. I felt like a widow. My husband, the man I knew before alcohol and drugs took over, is gone. He is simply gone. I am grieving the man I loved so fucking much. At the same time, the addict that currently inhabits his body is still very much alive. I know this because I witness it daily. I grapple with the loss of the person I once knew, while feeling rage towards the addict he has become. This situation, and the accompanying grief, make me feel crazy — truly crazy. I'm mourning my lover and am torn by his addiction and lies. Yet, I push forward for the sake of my son and myself; it's all I can do.

For once, I was able to recognize the vast dissonance: the person's body was physically present but emotionally devoid, like a zombie. I felt as though I was being subjected to a therapeutic approach called "flooding." In this technique, an individual is thrust into the pinnacle of an anxiety-triggering scenario, without any means to soften its impact. Typically, this technique is used for people with phobias, with the goal of extinguishing the negative reaction to a situation completely. So, I found myself an unwilling participant in this overwhelming process, with no relief in sight. The fact is that I don't know for sure if he'll ever emotionally occupy his body again; therefore, the flooding technique will only have a negative effect on me. This is the complexity of grief when loving an addict.

My dear friend Yvette witnessed this in her own mother. When Yvette's brother became an addict, he transformed from the man who once adored his mother into a stranger; though he was still alive, it was as if he was no longer present on this Earth. With pain in her eyes, Yvette recalled how her mother would cry. Yvette described how she would plead with her mother: "Mom, he's not dead! You're acting like he died." Her mother replied, "He has died. He is not the same. I'm grieving my son."

After some reflection, I decided to begin preparing for my husband's funeral by writing his eulogy. This was a way for me to release the pain of facing a harsh reality: that the man I once knew might never return. I booked a night alone in a hotel. I needed space, primarily because the guilt of expressing my sadness in front of my son was overwhelming, but also because I knew I needed to give myself permission to grieve.

"We gather here today to remember the life of my husband and father of our son. While T's mind and spirit are no longer with us, his physical body still walks this Earth. Today, we acknowledge and honor his mind and spirit, which made me fall in love with him.

T was a gentle man who loved plants, animals, and insects. He was always quick to rescue a spider, gently cupping it in his hands and allowing it to crawl up his arm before releasing it. We connected over our shared love of animals. He lovingly treated Reese, our Mini Aussie, like his own child shortly after I returned to New York, following our two years of long-distance during my time in grad school. He enjoyed caring for her, creating a special bowl structure for her food, and becoming incredibly tender when she'd playfully wiggle her tail at him. He had a unique way of communicating with her, using specific sounds that would make Reese playfully roll over, eager to shower him with affection.

T loved the woods and thrived in nature; he was in his element when he was making fires and playing Frisbee. He was an avid chess player and won an impromptu chess game to impress me during our first date. He did impress me, along with his attentiveness to my needs and especially with his humor. We enjoyed simple nights at home where I was the audience to his daily standup routine. I was his biggest fan, lucky to be in the front row. T was so quick, so smart with his comedy. He would use his long stature to assist him, often bending his arms and moving his body like a velociraptor.

T was a handy man with humor. He was always helping me out in creative ways. For example, he cut holes in my sports bra right where my nipples would be, so I could pump milk for our son hands-free. T was so proud to be a father and often wore our son in a baby carrier while doing the dishes. We loved to sleep together as a family. T would often put our son between us because our son felt too far away from him when he was snoozing in his crib. T and our son have the same body structure, which contributes to their ability to scale any wall or structure (if you know, you know), T's love of climbing lives on in his son.

T, thank you for the good years because there were many. Thank you for our boy, and who you were will not be forgotten. We will always love you. See you on the other side."

Grief Will Always Find You

I'm alone with our son, who has just crawled into bed with me. His body is pressed tightly against mine, with his arm snuggled around my neck. As I try to gently move my son to make more room for myself, I accidentally knock over my cup of water on the bedside table. It never fails. I always seem to drop or spill things. I skillfully move to the floor without making noise, feeling around for the laundry basket in the darkness, remembering that I just threw a dirty towel in before bed. On my hands and knees cleaning up my mess, I am unsure if all the water is gone. Frustrated, I feel around the bed for my phone to shed some light. As I search, I pause. There is a notable dip in the mattress pad where my body had just lay. I flatten my hand, slowly moving it from side to side. I can't believe how indented it has become. "You can really feel the shape of my body," I think to myself. After confirming the floor is dry, I decide to walk to the other side of the bed since moving my son is clearly too much. I lift the blankets, expecting to sink into the bed, but it remains firm with no dip. Since the beginning of our relationship, my husband and I have each claimed a specific side of the bed: I'm on the left, and he's on the right. Laying here, I'm immersed in the odd sensation of being on his side and wonder why it took me so long to switch. It's as if we remained on our designated sides, holding onto hope that he would choose us over the bottle in the basement.

My son cries out and reaches over to where I was just lying, noticing that I'm not in my usual spot. I reassure him that I'm still here by taking his hand

and placing it on my face. Seconds later, I feel his body twitch, signaling that he's fallen back asleep. Since he was a baby, whenever he slept between us, he would spread his arms out and examine our faces, feeling the outline of our noses and mouths to ensure he was still with us. It was such a sweet sensation that we both loved. The memory washes over me, and I begin to weep.

I cry, realizing he no longer reaches out to both sides of the bed. I count back in my head and realize it's been months since the three of us slept together as a family. The pain of this memory overtakes me. It feels like someone is slowly shaving off the skin above my heart.

Memories pour down on me, and flashes of our marriage counseling sessions start to hit me, filling me with sadness. I can't determine whether I'm awake, half-awake, or in a full-on nightmare. I'm now sitting next to my husband, though we aren't looking at each other. I can smell his cologne, which he uses to mask the alcohol. As he speaks, I distinctly hear—or remember hearing—my husband describing how he had become "bored" in life, a feeling which the marriage therapist said was common.

At the moment, it feels as if the memory is being replayed verbatim, but the difference is that I now have a sword. Every time he says "bored," I grab the sword and stab it quickly into my chest. No one notices the blood leaking from me. No one is at all concerned with my pain. I try to speak, but I can't. They both carry on. As the therapist describes how addiction can change the pleasure receptors in the brain, providing him with context around why he feels this way, I just stare down at the sword in my chest. It's painless, so I slowly twist the blade around as if it's a game, and then look out the window in a daydream.

My son wakes again pulling me into the present world. I can tell that sleeping in the spot saved for Daddy is throwing him off, so I pick him up and move him to the other side of me so that we are both lying where Daddy once was. He touches my face again, and moments later, he's calm.

With this sweet little boy and his gentle hands touching my face, giving me so much comfort and love, I agonize over the question: *how could he ever be bored of this?* Sorrow and anger rise from deep within my being. *How could he take this for granted?* I think I'm drifting back to my nightmare when I find myself grabbing the sword from my chest, feeling proud of my open wound as blood gushes out.

I get on a chariot and fly at an enormous speed, pointing my sword forward into the darkness and screaming at the top of my lungs. The scene I experience is reminiscent of *Mad Max*. My hair is coming off my head from the sheer speed, my eyes bulge, and I continue fearlessly into the abyss. My movements and painful sobs, which have increased in volume, awaken me. I fumble with my phone, eventually activating the white noise app. I crank up the volume, ensuring I don't disturb my son as I finish my wailing. I'm too weak to make it to the bathroom to cry. My body convulses in bed until I'm too exhausted to cry anymore. Then, I drift off as blood soaks the bed and my clothes.

By morning, I woke to find my hair wet, and my clothes stuck to me from sweat. I also noticed that both of us had gravitated back to the left side of the bed.

Reflection Time

Grief is a significant part of the healing process when you love an addict. The person you love and cherish has succumbed to his or her addiction. Take a moment now to acknowledge all the wonderful aspects of the person to whom you didn't have a chance say goodbye: the person before addiction took its toll. If this is too hard for you in this moment, feel free to skip this section.

If you feel ready, begin to write a eulogy below. For some of you, you may have already had to do this for real, and to those individuals, I offer my deepest, *deepest* condolences. If the addict you love has died, you likely felt unprepared - after all, how can anyone be prepared?

So for those of us still existing with a body that once housed the spirit of the person you love, please give yourself the space to acknowledge *everything* that they were. You and they deserve that honor.

In Honor of _______________

CHAPTER THREE

Acceptance is a Bitch

To regain some ownership over my life after recognizing that I had become entrenched in the addictions of my loved ones, I utilized the therapeutic approach called Acceptance and Commitment Therapy (ACT) on myself (more on that later). I had always worked with therapists who mainly employed CBT (Cognitive Behavioral Therapy), DBT (Dialectical Behavior Therapy), or a mixture of both. Still, my new friend and colleague, Tonya, mentioned that her primary treatment modality was ACT. I was unfamiliar with the ACT therapeutic approach, and since I admired and respected her so much, I decided to take the workshop she organized in the fall of 2019.

When I attended the first day of a three-day workshop on ACT, I was skeptical. Nothing seemed direct. I was expecting some generic role-plays on how to change behavior. Instead, the presenter spoke in metaphors and asked questions that cut deep, *too deep* for my liking. I was more emotional than I ever expected and irritated because of this. I assumed I'd zone out during the presentation and pass silly notes to my colleague and friend, Melissa, to see if I could make her laugh during quiet moments (I clearly love being mischievous). I imagined I'd just sip on coffee all weekend, quickly obtain my CEUs (Continuing Education Units), and maintain my license with the state of New York. I was so wrong, and I kept screaming in my head, "Why are you making me feel, damn it? I didn't pay nearly $400 to have swollen eyes by the end of the weekend!"

During the workshop, I was encouraged to assess my values and how I was possibly not acting consistently with them. The presenter was not instructing me on how to change my harmful or destructive thoughts; there was no talking through my feelings; instead, he asked me to *sit* with my feelings because pain and discomfort are a "fact of life." Fuck. My chin started to quiver. This always happens before losing it; it signals that I AM NOT OKAY. I was, at a workshop with colleagues/friends, and I was about to full-on ball my eyes out. I wanted to learn how to help THEM, the "others," NOT me.

During an exercise in which I had to maintain eye contact with Melissa and focus on a memory from my past, I finally broke down. Initially, I distracted myself, acting silly and making faces at Melissa. However, anger soon welled up within me, sadness lurked behind it, and I finally surrendered. I wasn't actively suppressing these overwhelming emotions; I simply couldn't hold them back anymore. Fuck it. I decided to embrace and feel them fully. ACT emphasizes mindfulness, which is essentially a fancy way of saying that you are in a mental state of awareness. This meant I had to *feel the feelings* in my physical body. I could greet my pain instead of escaping through distractions, even though I often wanted to. Every second felt like an hour, but after the first day, I felt somewhat elevated, as if something within me had been released.

At the workshop, I was encouraged to reflect on my deepest desires and cultivate awareness. I began to truly understand that I have a say in how I treat myself and the world. I had choices, and I created a list of facts based on what I learned:

1. You are only responsible for yourself.
2. Setting boundaries is an act of love towards both you and the other person.
3. You don't have to live in a place that feels unpredictable and unsafe.
4. If you ignore your pain and continue enabling, you aren't being a loving partner or friend to either them or yourself.
5. Addiction is a genuine response — it stems from trauma and pain. That same pain can hurt you. Protect yourself and remember that their pain has nothing to do with their love for you.

§

Bittersweet Symphony: Singing to Myself

Why are you using a song title as a subheading?

Let me explain. ACT is a therapeutic approach that embodies the spirit of "bittersweet". I have long loved this word because it is both an oxymoron and a paradox. And while the lyrics from the song "Bitter Sweet Symphony" constantly played in my head, I never actually delved past the title until recently. I've always been too entranced by the song's beautiful, sweet, and relaxing violin sound. Yet, the song's content is *far* from sweet and relaxing. It possesses a nonchalant bitterness and rawness, full of truth. This realization made me feel seen to my marrow.

Given that the song is best experienced with the windows down and volume turned up high, I won't make you read through the lyrics. I implore you to listen and sit with the message I believe it conveys.

The song's meaning is debated. However, many recognize its theme of powerlessness — the overwhelming weight of life dominated by circumstances beyond our control. We often grapple, whether consciously or unconsciously, with that powerlessness, yearning for freedom and meaning. Some suggest that the song alludes to the rules and regulations of the world and the games we must play to succeed. But all I hear is the voice of someone who loves an addict.

The imagery of a rigid mold speaks to the limits that the narrator, Richard Ashcroft, experiences, but it isn't from a lack of ability, intelligence, imagination, or flexibility. Instead, the mold feels like a prison; one can see possibilities through the prison bars, but for now, one is stuck.

One can feel the desperation and envision a loved one of an addict lying on the floor, wailing from the pain. As the weight of reality sets in, they reach a point of acceptance. They understand that curing the addiction is not their responsibility. Yet, this acceptance brings with it a profound sense of loneliness. This is what it means to sit in pain, *truly* feeling it.

The song deeply resonates with those who love an addict. At times, you can feel as if you are no longer an autonomous person, as if you've lost your agency. However, you come to realize that this experience, in fact, does not have to take ownership of your life.

During the mid-90s, before the song was released, the band The Verve agreed to pay a small fee to use a five-note sample from the relatively unpopular song "The Last Time" by the Rolling Stones. Ironically, this song was heavily inspired by "This May Be the Last Time" by the Staple Singers, an American gospel, soul, and R&B group. In 1997, "Bitter Sweet Symphony" was released and became a huge hit. I remember watching the music video at my friend's house, since my parents had MTV removed from our cable, deeming it "inappropriate" and "sinful." This only intensified my desire to watch it. I especially enjoyed seeing the lead singer bump into the shoulders of random strangers on the street as he sang along to the ethereal tune.

After seeing the song's success, Allen Klein, the former manager of the Rolling Stones, filed a lawsuit against The Verve. He argued that they had used a larger sample of the original piece than permitted. This claim seemed absurd, as The Verve had used exactly what they had agreed to. The song was unrecognizable from the sample, and not a single lyric was written by the Rolling Stones. The work was entirely that of Richard Ashcroft, the lead singer of The Verve. Nevertheless, the case went to court. Since the Rolling Stones had ample time and resources to engage in a prolonged legal battle and potentially profit from the song's success, The Verve capitulated. Faced with a daunting legal challenge and the risk of losing more money than they had earned, The Verve relinquished 100 percent of their royalties from the song to the Rolling Stones. Consequently, The Verve didn't earn a single cent from the song for 22 years. Ashcroft created this beautiful song, but the bitterness of greed deprived him of its rewards.

Why are you explaining the trivia around this song?

Just stay with me; I swear it'll make sense.

Ok, proceed...

In April 2019, Mick Jagger and Keith Richards signed over all their songwriting credits and publishing rights to Richard Ashcroft. No one knows precisely why Jagger & Richards decided to surrender these credits and rights, but Ashcroft described this turn of events in his statement as "remarkable and life-affirming." The following month, Ashcroft was rightfully honored with the Novello Award for Outstanding Contribution to British Music from the British Academy of Songwriters, Composers, and Authors.

Oh, I see the parallels now.

Good. Ashcroft lived exactly what he narrated in the song. He was like the loved one of an addict, the superstar version. Rather than falling into the pitfalls of blame, he embodied the sentiments of ACT. He accepted his powerlessness against forces greater than himself and, while maintaining his integrity and dignity, was validated in a more meaningful way than he could have imagined, making it all so "bittersweet."

Reflection Time

There is so much healing to be found when you sit in stillness and don't run away from your emotions. We have been conditioned to view negative emotions as external problems that we must eliminate. In reality, the more we avoid these emotions, the worse they can become. I recommend doing a guided meditation to help you gain awareness. Below, you will find a meditation I often utilize.

§

Find a comfortable position with your feet on the floor, back straight.

Allow your shoulders to lower and loosen.

Unlock your jaw.

Close your eyes or fix them on a spot at a 45-degree angle.

For the next few minutes, set your intention to simply be present, sitting in the here and now.

Have an attitude of openness and curiosity.

Bring your awareness to any sensations you may be experiencing.

Simply notice this without judging, analyzing, or trying to change it.

You are safe to feel.

You are safe to observe.

Observe with curiosity.

Thoughts will come into your awareness.

Allow them to come and freely, let them go.

Tell yourself again and again that these thoughts can come and go as they please.

Do not try to hold on to them or push them away.

The thoughts are like clouds that you are just observing; they are just passing by.

You do not have to attach to any one thought-cloud, just watch it pass by.

Simply acknowledge their presence and let them be.

From time to time, urges, feelings and sensations will probably arise.

When they do, simply notice them, and let them be.

Welcome them.

You can pull out a chair for them and let each one have a seat at your table.

They are allowed to be here.

Make room for them.

Let them stay or let them go as they please.

Do not keep them from coming or going; just observe them.

From time to time, your attention may "wander off."

When this happens, it's okay.

Kindly acknowledge it.

Just observe it.

Do not attach any label to this distraction.

Just gently acknowledge it.

Grant yourself compassion in this moment.

It is okay to feel.

This is a skill that takes time.

You are building the skill of awareness.

You are allowing your feelings and sensations to emerge.

You are safe.

Now, begin to bring yourself back into the room.

Notice where you are.

Notice your awareness of yourself.

Notice that it can all exist at the same time.

When you are ready, open your eyes.

You are here.

You are present.

The End

Congrats! You just finished the meditation. Take a moment to reflect on your experience and write it down.

____
____
____
____
____
____
____
____

If you are not too worn out from the meditation, take a moment to reflect and answer the following questions:

> When you hear the word "acceptance," what comes to mind?

____
____
____
____
____
____
____
____

> Did you relate to Richard Ashcroft? Why or why not?

____
____
____
____
____
____
____

What songs do you feel embody your experience of loving an addict?

____

____

____

____

____

____

____

____

Now, choose one song that is your #1. Use the space below to write out the lyrics of this song and analyze it. Dive deep into your analysis? If you need some guidance, consider the following:

What verse(s) or lyric(s) affects you the most? Think about the *emotions*. What emotions are being evoked? Journal what comes up.

What is the tempo of the song? Meaning – is it fast or slow? How does the tempo make you feel? Take note of this.

What is the texture of the song? Meaning – what types of sounds do you hear? How does the texture make you feel? Write it down.

What about the timbre? Meaning – what kind of character or quality of the musical sounds does the song have? Are they smooth, breathy, rough, smoky, flat? How does it make you feel? Does the timbre evoke any emotion in you? Just become aware and write down anything that speaks to you."

CHAPTER FOUR
Don't

Don't Judge Til You're in DAG

In my house growing up, the focus on my sister's addiction was obsessive, to the point that the constant analyzing by my family was expected not once, but several times a day. In my mind, I coined it the "Daily Analyzing Group," or DAG for short, since it consisted of hours of mental chess. We'd go over what could happen, how to stop it, how to intervene, how my sister might react, how we'd then react to each possible reaction and so on. The DAG went from tolerable to painful. Sometimes when the analyzing cycle began, I could feel my irritation rising, heart pounding, and pressure in my ears so intense that I felt my eardrums might explode and splatter blood all over the room if I heard "why is she…" or "how can we…" one more time. I realize that this might sound overly dramatic. However, every single discussion, EVERY moment, revolved around preventing my sister from basically killing herself with drugs. Now, as I read this, I think to myself "just leave then, stop being a part of it, dummy!" but at the time, I did not think that was an option. I felt that leaving would be a betrayal to my family and a disappointment to my mother. Even worse, I feared it would leave her to cope alone, especially as my dad often sought escape on the golf course.

One sunny day in a Walmart parking lot, my aunt learned about the depressing state of my sister's addiction. Things had gone so far off track that my mother was finally confiding in outside people. I'm somewhat ashamed to admit this—though not completely—but I once muttered, "It would be so much easier if she weren't here." I will never forget the look of horror on my aunt's face, a mix of shock and disgust at my statement. She asked how I could say such a thing, and I remember replying, "I don't know."

I have many clients who have confided in me, sharing their profound shame for even harboring the thought of wishing it would all go away. They wish the misery would end, or sometimes they wish the addict wasn't alive to continue causing havoc. Many are surprised when I tell them, "I have felt that way, too." I share my own feelings to normalize such reactions and help them understand that it's not unusual for the brain to have these thoughts. In fact, the brain is trying to *protect you* by allowing you to fantasize about different escape scenarios. If you have such thoughts, it's an indicator that you've taken on too much and it's time to step back. These thoughts signal underlying mental anguish, so be gentle with yourself.

My aunt was just learning about the situation, whereas I had been living it for months and months. She wasn't yet a part of DAG, but I knew that if she were initiated into DAG and became an active member as long as I have, she would likely echo the same sentiments.

The truth is, you can't really judge people when you haven't weathered their storm. People may accuse you of not "doing more" or being cruel, but you must trust in your deep understanding of your own limitations. When people question or critique you, either think "fuck off" or offer a snide, Southern "bless your heart."

Don't Be a Bitter Bitch

You are sitting in your car outside of Trader Joe's, trying to motivate yourself to run errands, but you find yourself crying unexpectedly. You wonder when the antidepressants you were prescribed will start to quell the constant worrying thoughts and the feeling of being on edge. Your moods have been shifting; moments of intense rage give you a chilling insight into the mindset of arsonists. Right now, you decide to step out of the car, popping on a pair of shades to hide your swollen eyes. As you slowly stroll past the gluten-free breakfast options, you glance up to see a few customers laughing with their companions. Under your breath, you mutter, "Oh, isn't your life so fucking perfect?" One person looks back and you realize they may have heard you. Oh no, here comes the shame. You wonder, "*Who have I become?*" You never used to be so hateful and mean. There was a time when things were easier, but when was that? You stare into the distance, trying to recall when you last felt *genuinely* happy. Was it just last year? What has changed?
It hits you. When they started using, that's when you stopped being happy.

Oh shit. There it is. There's no denying it anymore.

See, addiction does you dirty. You know it's there but it's easier to look away. Either way, it's hell until you wake up. Waking up is NOT easy. It's fucking brutal.

I've had many nicknames for myself during this time, but "Bitter Bitch" was the most fitting. I even took up cross-stitching for stress reduction. However, my husband was confused when I showed him my piece that read, "Fold Your Worries Into Paper Planes and Turn Them Into Flying Fucks." My son was an early reader, and while this art piece brought me joy, I'm ashamed that I introduced him to his first curse word.

When you step out of the darkness of denial, you experience relief. However, you now must confront what you previously avoided. That means owning up to your role and acknowledging your ugliness. How do you do that? It is acceptance, forgiveness, and hard work. You may have new definitions for those words.

While listening to a podcast, author Ashley C. Ford was asked about her definition of forgiveness. Her answer has stuck with me. She said, "Forgiveness is letting go of the idea of how it was supposed to be." Damn. Preach!

Don't Let the Addict Make You an Addict

Let's discuss self-medicating, Seeking escape this way can be tempting, because it provides a reprieve from reality, but one must keep an eye on that shit. If my point is not clear, let me illustrate with an example:

During the peak of my husband's addiction, I found solace in "sleep shopping." I would just pop a tiiiiny piece of Xanax and begin browsing online. On the surface, it might seem harmless. As I mindlessly scrolled through Instagram, targeted ads would pop up, tailored precisely to my tastes and desires. It felt as though the masters of the internet genuinely understood and cared for me, suggesting that material purchases could bring me peace. I was going through hell, so I figured I deserved a little "pick-me-up," right? Wrong!

I'd wake to several boxes on my doorstep, and it felt like Christmas. I'd get giddy like a little kid because I genuinely did not know what was in those boxes. Let me repeat, I truly did not know what was in them. I'd rip them open with delight, but there was a 50/50 chance that the excitement I craved would quickly dissipate when I realized what I had bought. Toeless yoga socks? Eww! Salt and pepper shakers from Anthropologie? Pass. Bootyband from Amazon? Ok, keep. At first, indulging in the delusion that a plump ass would make it all better was fun. Then, it stopped being fun because I was spending way more time at the post office returning items than I'd like to admit. One time, I had over $600 in returns. I would say, "ugh, this is like an addiction"... umm, yeah, it's an addiction.

The shopping was one thing, but the Xanax was worse. It was a temporary escape, and even though it was prescribed to me, I would still take small pieces in a way it was not intended. It's very effective when I have to fly; I can sleep the night before and stay calm while on the plane.

After using it semi-consistently for three weeks, I observed that it no longer alleviated my sadness as it once did, and the nightly clenching of my jaw intensified. After waking to a pounding headache and more returns, I realized it was all becoming too much. I am lucky that I could just put the Xanax away and stop when I recognized the issue. When I took this step, I began to grasp the situation and stopped distracting myself from reality. So when I say, "Don't let the addict make you an addict," I'm referring to the resistance against numbing oneself or becoming addicted as a way to ignore another's addiction.

Don't Get Mad, Get Everyone

One night after getting my son to bed and settling into my "sleep scrolling" routine, I came across my friend Malaika's Instagram story. There, she commented on her deep sadness over the loss of actor Michael K. Williams, famous for his role in "The Wire," who had died from an apparent heroin overdose. Along with her condolences, she gave a message of support to his loved ones, who would be forever impacted by the tremendous loss brought about by the destruction of addiction.

I sat up immediately. My mind raced. The wording signaled that I was not alone. I felt it in my bones – "Malaika loves an addict." I whispered to myself, "She knows this kind of pain; I know it."

I met Malaika in the winter of 2017 at a yoga retreat in Mexico. Attending the retreat was intimidating since I was a novice yogi. However, it offered an escape from the harsh NYC winter for me and a group of girlfriends. Despite being broke, I decided to put the cost on a credit card because I knew I needed it. In addition, as a new therapist, I was burnt out from working non-stop to obtain the clinical hours necessary for full licensure. I attended to keep my head above water, while Malaika was there to co-lead the retreat with our mutual friend.

When introduced to her, I was met with kind, deep chocolate eyes; her presence filled the room. She was gentle and centered, yet oozing confidence—not in a cocky way, but in a self-assured, "I know who I am" kind of way. I imagine she came out of the womb as a little Buddha baby, all-knowing and wise. She conducted a guided meditation, and her voice sounded like a lullaby from my childhood, so calming and maternal. She felt like a creature sent here to soothe us all. She was—and still is—a Goddess.

After the retreat, we kept in contact through Instagram, messaging each other here and there. However, I mainly admired her from afar, feeling slightly envious of her life. She lived in a beautiful historic home, had a thriving yoga and doula practice, and started a lovely family with her partner. Yet, at the same time, what she posted on Instagram wasn't just for show. She was vulnerable about her life and challenges with motherhood and relationships. She often encouraged honesty and authenticity in the virtual space and in our personal lives.

My sudden revelation about her loving an addict was confirmed when I messaged her in response to her post. I could never have expected her response though:

> *"I'm leaving my marriage because of it. 2+ years of addiction was enough to do more than enough damage. Al-Anon has been a divine gift for my soul and sanity."*

"WHAT??!" I responded.

No. There is NO WAY the Goddess could be experiencing this! She's too sacred!

She shared that she now runs an Al-Anon meeting every Wednesday. She provided me with the Zoom link and four Excel spreadsheets, listing all the meetings available every day across four different time zones. She explained that this flexibility allows her to join West Coast meetings if she can't attend one during her regular hours. She recommended that I attend five different meetings to find the one that best suits my "vibe", which I truly appreciated.

My judgment and stereotypes about the kind of people I imagined I'd encounter at an Al-Anon meeting were quickly dispelled—I envisioned an old crusty cat lady smoking a cigarette for some reason—but I met people of all ages and genders. From badass bosses to studious college-aged individuals, some were shy, some outgoing, and others had BDE, a confident presence, which I deeply appreciated. They encouraged me to keep attending, highlighting the significance of a supportive community where you can share both your challenges and triumphs. In these meetings, it's not about the addict; it's about *you*, the loved one. You receive the attention, care, and resources that the addict typically gets, allowing you to cope with the unwelcome intrusions in your life and conquer the disease that has affected you.

Substance abuse is a disease that does not just affect the addict; it also impacts everyone around them. It's often labeled as a family disease. It was then that I finally grasped why Malaika runs a group. Initially, I wondered why she would want to associate herself with anything related to addiction again after all she had endured, especially as she was ending her marriage. However, I realized that we, like her, had become sick as well. The drawings in Chapter 2, labeled "The Overwhelm," symbolize this sickness. When an addict acts out, we react. While we all respond to the addict, we frequently fall into a pattern—a subconscious tug-of-war for control, aiming to restore balance. Through Al-Anon, one can learn to let go of the rope and opt out of the tug-of-war. It's a reminder to concentrate on one's own life, emphasizing that *everyone* has choices—choices in how we react and choices in how we live.

When you research the "family disease of addiction," you'll find a breakdown of the roles people play in the disease. Typically, there are 5 or 6 common roles. I'm going to explain them first and then talk shit about them:

The Addict – the focal point of everyone.

The Caretaker – the enabler; the person who hides the addict's problems.

The Hero – the person who tries to create order by being overly responsible and self-sufficient.

The Scapegoat – the person who acts out in an attempt to divert attention from the addict's behavior.

The Mascot – the comedian; the person who uses humor or silliness to lessen the stress of the addict's behavior.

The Lost Child – the person who quietly flies under the radar while everyone else plays their roles.

I understand this breakdown is helpful in some ways, but it's too simplified and does not acknowledge the complexity of the disease. I wish there was a disclaimer for people that reads:

These roles can overlap and shift overtime; they are not locked in time.

I mention this because I assumed many of these roles at different points and sometimes held more than one simultaneously. For example, during the time of my sister's addiction in high school, I first joined my parents in "The Enabler" role but quickly became "The Hero." I primarily played the role of "The Hero." However, I occasionally shifted to "The Mascot" as well. I liked to divert attention from my sister by being silly and trying to make my mom laugh. At the same time, I excelled academically to gain my father's attention and deflect from the situation.

These roles became so ingrained in me, and the disease spread throughout my being. Even during the roughly 10 years when there were no addicts in my life, I never let go of these roles. So, the reason Malaika continues to attend Al-Anon and why I continue to get support is the same, we recognize that we can easily slip back into our old “roles” since they are so ingrained in us, and we know that we do not have to be alone in this journey.

Reflection Time

Have you ever fantasized about the ways in which your situation with the addict could change?

Have you ever had thoughts that you are ashamed to admit?

How do you feel learning that your brain is protecting you?

When these thoughts begin to occur, it is important to recognize that what you are going through is *very* hard. Give yourself permission to recognize that this is hard. Say it with me: "This is hard."

If you need reminding, below I have provided two permission slips that you can cut out and hang as a reminder. I created two options: one for those who don't like profanity or have kids around, and one for those who feel a release every time they yell "fuck!"

§

I, _________, give myself permission to recognize that loving an addict is hard. I did not ask for this! I may have unwanted thoughts or feelings, but it's just my body's way of protecting me, because, again, *this is hard!*

Signature: ____________________ Date:________

§

I, ___________, give myself permission to recognize that loving an addict is fucking HARD. I did not ask for this! Unwanted thoughts or feelings may come up but it's just my body's way of protecting me because THIS IS SO FUCKING HARD!

Signature: ____________________ Date:________

§

You might realize you're different due to various internal changes, such as feeling continual sadness, hopelessness, anxiety, hypersensitivity, denial, or anger. There comes a moment, or a gradual recognition, that finally clicks in your mind. You may have been distracted from the true culprit of your change: your loved one's addiction.

At what moment did you realize that you were being impacted by their addiction?

____

____

____

____

____

____

What emotions come up when you reflect on this moment?

____

____

____

____

____

____

Take a moment to think about acceptance and forgiveness. What comes up for you?

____

____

____

____

____

____

Give yourself permission to define these words for yourself. Here are some examples:

Acceptance:

- Recognizing the truth in my life.
- Coming to terms with the fact that I have no control over another person.
- Releasing judgment of my life and how things "should" be instead of how they really are.

Forgiveness:

- An action to release the weight of resentment toward the addict.
- Freeing yourself by no longer harboring negative feelings even though those negative feelings are warranted.
- Acknowledging that things do not have to be the way I envisioned them in my head.

What is your definition of acceptance?

____

____

____

____

____

What is your definition of forgiveness?

____

____

____

____

____

Have you ever found yourself numbing, distracting, escaping, or self-medicating? If so, can you identify the trigger?

____

Is this in reaction to the addict's behavior?

Is reaction helpful or harmful to you?

What can you do to genuinely distract yourself instead of simply acting on an urge? If you need suggestions, consider the following:

-Plant flowers
-Scream at the sky
-Break some cardboard boxes
-Take an exercise class
- Write down your feelings (and burn them if needed)
-Listen to music
-Call a friend
-Attend an Al-Anon or Nar-Anon meeting

Things I Can Do to Distract

When did you first disclose to another person that you were struggling with loving an addict?

What did you feel when you did this? How was it received?

Think back to the roles listed. Which ones do you identify with? Which ones have your family members or friends filled? Write your responses next to the roles below:

The Caretaker

The Hero

The Scapegoat

The Mascot

The Lost Child

Take a moment to review what you wrote. Did these roles evolve or change over time?

If you are a visual person, you can make a Venn diagram of the roles, and if you want to dig *really* deep, you can make a Venn diagram for each month or year that your roles changed or overlapped. it's okay if the shifts happened often. There's no need to judge; just bring awareness to it.

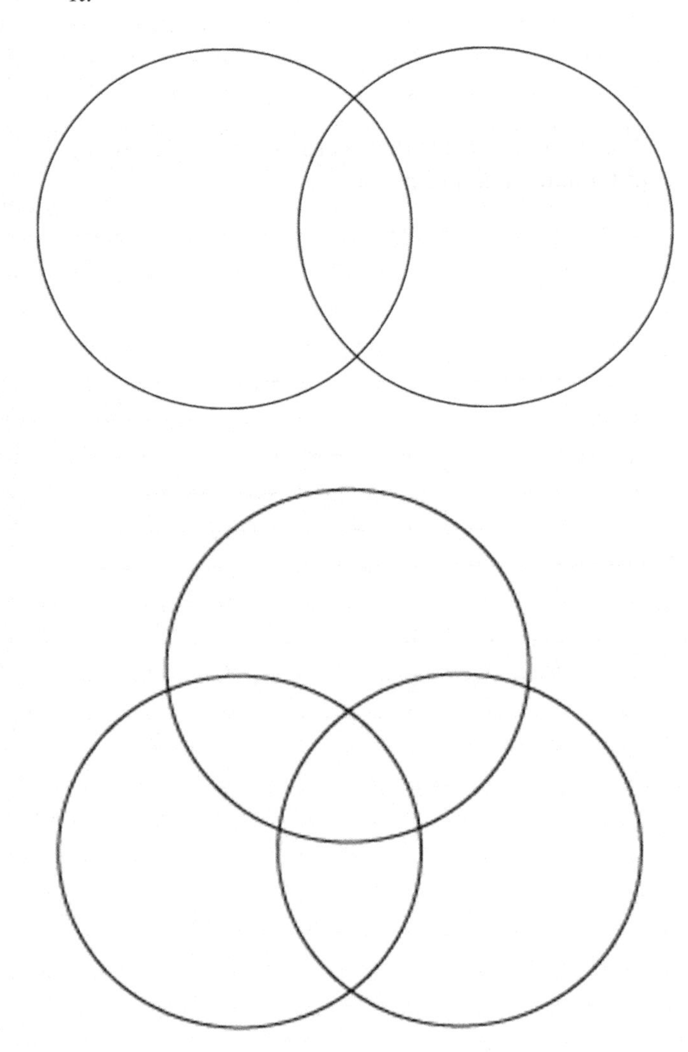

How do you feel about these roles now that you have acknowledged them?

Are there any roles that were not covered? If so, put a name and definition to it.

CHAPTER FIVE

Stop Yourself & Parent Yourself

The Cycle

Before my husband's addiction reached a crescendo, I spent many days ashamed of myself. I had not yet learned that you should never, and I mean NEVER, have a serious discussion or make even the slightest comment to someone under the influence. It's like explaining to your best friend how to file taxes when they wake up from anesthesia after removing their wisdom teeth. They likely won't remember or even comprehend what you are saying to them, but they may be delusional enough to say some shit that frustrates you. I often found myself in this predicament in the evenings with my husband. I would approach him to discuss the state of his addiction. In response, he would usually use tactics like deflecting or denying the issue. Often, he would tell me I was wrong, claim I took it too personally, and then I'd begin to yell, curse, or shut down completely. I'd end up being the worst parts of myself. He might or might not remember the next day, leaving me confused and with yet another thing to process.

Since I couldn't bear another day of feeling like shit, I decided to try a new approach to communicate with him (when I still believed I could). We are both somewhat artistic people, so I began drawing pictures of different scenarios, hoping he'd recognize the dysfunction. I'd spend my evenings creating these drawings, saving them for a time when he could truly "see" what was happening.

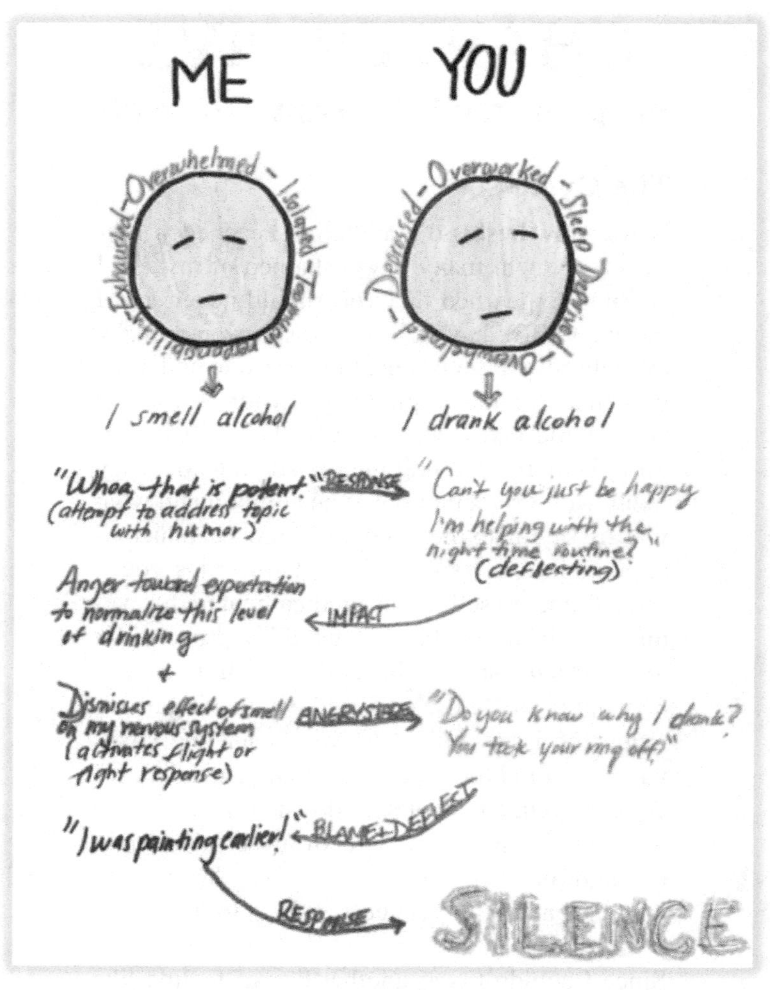

If I stand back and look at my behavior through a clinical lens, a mix of things were happening beyond what I was trying to express – themes of trauma, attachment, defense mechanisms, and emotional regulation.

Trauma Response/ Defense Mechanism

His behaviors mirrored my sister's at times, especially during her addiction, and activated my trauma response. I sought to correct the things I couldn't address as a teenager. Everything I wanted to say to my sister or parents during her addiction came out on my husband, which truly was not fair to him. I grew up in a household where you did not cuss. My mother always told me that I was smart enough to articulate myself without profanity. Even she would sometimes "spell cuss," such as "d-a-m-n-it" or "oh s-h-i-t." It was better if you spelled it and didn't actually say the word. Now that I'm an adult in my own home and marriage, if I wanted to express my feelings with a dash of profanity for flavor, d-a-m-n-it, I was going to! It could also be observed that I was utilizing the defense mechanism of displacement on him, meaning that I was projecting my past experience onto the present moment. Some of my reactions were not precisely because of him, but from what they activated from my past, and then I would act it out on him.

Attachment Styles/Co-Regulation

Another part of the problem was our difficulty in co-regulating. When people co-regulate, they can return their bodies, minds, and spirits to homeostasis, which is connected to calming a trauma response. The ability to self-regulate develops through interaction with caregivers such as parents and depends on predictable, responsive, and supportive environments. The three critical components of co-regulation needed during childhood are:

-A warm, responsive relationship where the child/young adult feels secure and cared for.

-An environment that buffers against excessive stress, enabling self-regulation to be both manageable and learned.

-Modeling or scaffolding of self-regulation through enactment between caregivers and the child/young adult.

While I would describe my childhood environment as fulfilling these needs, I would say that it changed during young adulthood, around the onset of my sister's addiction. As for my husband, he did not have any of these three components as a child. His mother left him and his sister when he was between 18 months old and three years old (we've heard varying time frames). His father's struggles with bipolar disorder contributed to neglect, a form of abuse that is not as overt as physical abuse and, therefore, more difficult to understand, it's silent but just as damaging. People who suffered from neglect as children will often have a hard time with self-worth and making strides in treatment. How do you identify and reflect on something that didn't happen?

Without secure attachments to our caregivers, people will struggle to co-regulate, thus affecting their healthy relationships. To heal this, we need to be in tune with our body and mind, which becomes very difficult when addiction and trauma are present. In Somatic Psychology, both the relational bond and limbic resonance serve as the ultimate healing functions. This concept might be challenging to grasp if you're not familiar with psychological theories; let's examine how this plays out in nature.

In the animal kingdom, animals have evolved to regulate themselves in critical situations, where they must either fight or flee to survive. Consequently, an animal that can manage its emotions is better equipped to survive in the wild. So, what am I getting at with this co-regulation and animal kingdom talk? I'm suggesting that if you aren't equipped to co-regulate, your relationships and personal life might become unsafe territories.

In such situations, one might be more likely to rely on addictions unless they learn to parent themselves. *Say what?* Yes, you will have to learn how to give *yourself* the guidance you should have been provided in childhood or young adulthood. To complicate matters further, having your own child might evoke feelings of loss and regret for the childhood you missed.

When things are hard, I know that I must make choices that are best for my son. I take pride in knowing our son will have experiences different from what my husband and I had. Yet, it's sometimes saddening to realize we won't share the same childhood memories as him. Nevertheless, it's essential to remember we can still provide what we missed out on. You can be the stable force, the reliable figure, and the embodiment of true unconditional love. You have the capacity to be the best parent to both yourself and your child.

To make this re-parenting real, I will look at a picture of myself as a child. In a certain childhood photo, I have strawberry blonde hair, crimped into a side ponytail, with bangs. My fair skin has an abundance of freckles splattered all over it.

My grandpa would say that they were marks of angel kisses. Kids at school and even my cousins would say they were from a cow that pooped on me. In reality, my skin simply had less melanin to begin with. Regardless of this freckle fact, I liked myself back then. I wasn't exposed to the world's cruelty; at least, I didn't understand it. I didn't know that I was poor because of my dad's lifelong illness. I also didn't realize that when my cousin commented about my family being on food stamps, it was a dig. Ignorance is bliss, I suppose. My point is, I love that little girl, and she still lives within me. I think of her when I start getting harsh about my inability to predict the future. I scroll back into my phone and see her. She's happy without makeup. She has hooded eyes that didn't require masterful concealing with a cat eye, as they weren't puffy from crying. She has spaces between her teeth that braces would eventually correct. Yet, she smiles easily, in contrast to the closed-lip smiles I currently give to hide my teeth and my shame. I begin feeling intense compassion for myself, which is empowering.

I eventually realized that I lacked the necessary support to learn how to regulate my emotions when I experienced distress around someone else's addiction. I stopped feeling sorry for myself and *took action*. I began to re-parent myself. I would write to myself the wise words I could imagine an elder speaking to me. I had to fight the urge to return to my old intervening patterns. This was so fucking hard, but it slowly began to work.

Here's an excellent example of a note I would leave for myself on my phone, on my computer, in my car, and on the bathroom mirror:

Read Before You Text

You will feel gross tomorrow because you spewed out mean and hurtful venom. Although you've been disrespected, it doesn't mean you must express your rage at this moment. Stop. Pause. Think. *Will this get me the change I desire?* Will this hurt me more due to a lack of sleep, feelings of lousiness tomorrow, or regret? Stop. This can be addressed tomorrow—calmly and from a loving place. Stay calm for your child; stay calm for yourself. You are responsible for your reactions. Should you *have to* demonstrate this level of self-restraint? No, but it will help you.

Reflection Time

Take a moment to reflect on your behaviors. How might your actions be connected to past trauma?

____

____

____

____

____

____

____

If nothing comes up for you in the trauma department, think about it: What types of defense mechanisms might you be using when dealing with an addict? I totally utilized "displacement," and my husband used "deflection." What do you use in difficult situations?

____

____

____

____

____

____

Think about your childhood. Did you have the type of environment that fostered co-regulation? If not, how has this manifested in your life? How has it impacted your ability to self-regulate?

____

____

____

____

____

____

How do you feel about possibly having to re-parent yourself?

Take a moment to create your own script to utilize when your emotions are running high. Talk to yourself as you would to a friend or elder. It's important to do this when you are not emotionally overwhelmed.

CHAPTER SIX
I am Portulaca

The Effects of the Facade

After dropping my son off at school on the second day of my husband's detox, I seemed fine on the outside. With a full face of makeup, I smiled at the school attendant and scurried off to my car as if I had somewhere important to go. I chose to take off work for fear that I would not be present for my patients, which was a wise choice because, when I got about a half-mile from the school, I parked the car and felt nothing. This numbness has been here before; *it feels familiar*. I think I developed this feeling when I was in DAG. I wince thinking about that period in my life and quickly try to help myself avoid that painful memory. A sharp pain crosses my chest as I realize that history is repeating itself.

I decided to try the coping skills I often help my patients develop; but... nothing, I draw a blank. *What do I even do? Where has my memory gone?* I know the answer: chronic stress.

Chronic stress is no fucking joke—it can straight up kill brain cells and shrink the prefrontal cortex, the part of the brain in charge of memory and learning. There's even data suggesting that chronic stress can shrink your entire brain. Fuck, that's not good. I genuinely think this is happening to me, and I feel like I'm getting dumber by the second. Fuck you, addiction! You've left me feeling like I have a pea-sized brain.

When my patients experience brain fog or memory loss similar to this, I usually explain that the brain can be compared to a computer. When there are too many windows open or programs running, it slows down because it's using a ton of memory.

To improve its performance, you have to close some programs and allow your brain to rest. Then I often hear, "But I can't even rest anymore; I don't even know what that is." Deciding to head back home, I ponder if lying in my bed might be the worst choice for me. "What do I even like to do? What gives me peace?"

I kept driving and pondering, forgetting what question I had asked myself. Then I'd remember it again; this probably happened three times. Everything looks so muddled outside my windshield, as if nature is just different variants of grey colors. Then, up on my left, I see my favorite plant nursery, and I quickly pull in. As I walked through the greenhouse, I felt my shoulders lower, my jaw loosen, and my whole body started relaxing just by being in this environment. While scanning the succulents and taking in their vibrant colors, I am drawn to what I later learn is called the Portulaca Mix. It has fleshy foliage and delicate blooming flowers; they look sweet and make me feel comforted. The woman working at the front desk tells me that it'll attract butterflies and honeybees. A dreamy vision fills my head, where I am sitting on a meditation pillow with butterflies surrounding me while I dip a honey dipper. Sure, this is unrealistic, but now I think, *"Yes, this is what I need."*

When I get home and pull out the big-ass tray of flowers, I realize that I didn't even ask about the care instructions for the plant, and I begin to chastise myself. In psychology, this is considered negative self-talk. Negative self-talk is your critical inner dialogue or excessive negativity (i.e., 'I'm an idiot, I'm so forgetful') that can lead you down the dark path of cognitive distortions (i.e., catastrophizing, blaming). It diminishes your confidence in yourself and your ability to make positive changes. When negative self-talk becomes habitual, it can alter your reality, creating an experience where you cannot succeed in any goals you set for yourself. It's a slippery slope, and I've witnessed the actual effects on my patients, family, and myself. I always strive to counteract its impact because I know the vital link between negative self-talk and decreased motivation, depression, and feelings of hopelessness – all the things I want to avoid. Unfortunately, my type of negative self-talk is that of a critical parent. Instead of reframing my thoughts using CBT or a positive statement to soothe this habit, I become a teenager and begin to yell at my internal critical parent: *"Aren't you tired of this? Can you just SHUT UP??"*

After this internal outburst, I remember that there are other ways to learn how to care for these plants, such as reading the plant care card that usually protrudes from the soil. So I look around and, aha! I find the slim, vertical plastic card! I wet my finger and brush the dirt aside so I can read the small print:

Portulaca Mix: Thrives under the worst conditions! Heat, drought, and poor soil seem to make these durable gems become even more colorful.

Tears fill my eyes as I shift between laughing and crying. But, of course, these are the flowers I chose! I sit down in my driveway, wiping snot away, and stare at the flowers. I love this message I so desperately needed today: Even in very shitty soil, beauty can unfold. I feel a moment of peace. If these stunning flower babies can thrive in the worst of the worst, maybe I can too. Even though I am foggy-headed, self-critical, and lethargic, I can perhaps thrive amidst the pain.

With mascara running down my cheeks, I feel the numbness fading a little, and a glimmer of hope emerges, with a deep knowing in my bones. My mantra is clear: I am Portulaca.

Self-Love ≠ Selfish

I couldn't believe how many gray hairs had sprouted during my husband's addiction. It felt like each day, I had white hair, popping from my middle part, and I couldn't believe my face: the line between my eyebrows had deepened, and the bags under my eyes were sharp and noticeable. Makeup would help, but I felt too tired to care for myself some days. Since my therapy sessions were online, I'd leave my sweats on, ensuring I was presentable from the waist up. I went through cans and cans of dry shampoo, as I found washing my hair a chore. I was always pretty good at keeping up with my hygiene and appearance, since it was instilled in me at a young age that this was important, but I just did not have the energy anymore. My mother would not leave the house without makeup, and I knew I would get approval and positive responses from them if I looked good; therefore, this was a big "no-no." But I didn't really care anymore. My son was good to go, and even my husband was well taken care of, but I looked like I got in a bad car wreck. Ironically, my massage therapist asked, "Were you in a car wreck?" I replied, "No," but she kept commenting on how something serious must have happened. Finally, I replied, "Well, I'm going through one of the hardest times in my life, so maybe that's it." She was quiet. "Fuck. "I have to take better care of myself," I thought.

When my husband finally went to rehab, my mother came to help out in the special way that only she can. Her way of loving herself and others was shown through physically moving and changing the environment – purging junk, rearranging furniture, and transforming spaces. This is when my mom comes alive. I love how she came in and transformed the house with so much enthusiasm, surprising me almost hourly with her changes, while I lay despondent in bed. She was filled with excitement for every item that I gave her permission to discard, whether through the trash or by shattering. My mom did bring me back to life by utilizing her unique trick to release the pain, which involves breaking. We chucked several glass vases at a concrete wall behind the garage.

Watching the vases explode was thrilling, a true release. We would comment on which vase made the best shatter sound and laugh. We would name a different glass or vase, specify what it represented, and then break the shit out of it. If there were plants in glass pots that had outgrown their containers, we would put on sunglasses, lay down a blanket, and take a hammer to them. We have videos documenting this, and I know we sound insane. I think this type of "therapy" is a family pastime. I remember hearing about how my cousins bought a bunch of Plaster of Paris figurines from a yard sale, lining them up on some stand outside to conduct target practice. They live in the country where shooting guns is as routine as brushing one's teeth. They learned from the best, since my aunt strapped my grandma's old walker to the back of her truck and drove down their rocky driveway until it was completely dismembered. There is something really therapeutic about watching something associated with a hard time get completely destroyed. It felt as if I could exert some control over the destruction, especially given how much the addict had already destroyed. My mom taught me this unique form of self-love.

Self-love is a state of appreciation for oneself that grows from actions that support our physical, psychological, and spiritual growth. When I held my well-being and happiness in high regard, I practiced self-love. I demonstrate self-love by taking care of my own needs and not sacrificing my well-being to please or serve others. Breaking shit and physically moving my body became a new form of self-love for me. It felt as if the trauma, the anger, the grief, and the sadness were moving through me and being released.

Granted, I didn't reach this realization on my own. My husband was in rehab, and I was given this brief moment in time to indulge. Oddly, I would often feel guilty or selfish when practicing self-love. When my option to step in and "save" the addict disappeared, I had to focus on myself. I began to parent myself; at first, I felt selfish. However, the more I honored myself, the more present I became, and I started to like myself again. If you ever question engaging in your form of self-love, please, I promise you, you are not selfish. You are doing exactly what you need to do.

Remember Who You Are

In the name of self-love, I decided to rotate the mattress on our bed. This decision was made with clarity. No more waiting; it was time to face the truth that my imprint would take his spot. I had risen to the occasion and existed as both mother and father, protector, and nurturer. The imprint was something to be proud of. It marked the one who stayed, chose to be a parent, and knew where I always belonged. The imprint no longer saddens me because it represents loyalty, responsibility, love, and devotion. I was always staying right by our child.

After I turned the mattress, I got my son on the bus, sat on the back porch, and enjoyed the morning chill. I grabbed a notepad and started to sketch while listening to the sound of birds in the tree overhead. *"Could life be this simple and calm?"* I thought to myself. My mind raced suddenly, signaling that there was danger or something I had forgotten, but no, there was nothing. There's only peace. And it felt so fucking gooood.

My friend Tim kept telling me that it made sense how I've been feeling on edge because I'm unsure of what my life will look like. I remember nodding to him and having a blank picture of my future. Was this what my life could look like? If so, I really liked the idea. Could my mornings be peaceful, a few days filled with my clients and other days available for rest, art, or writing? I thought that my current reality, which felt like I was wrapped in a warm, cozy weighted blanket, could be my every day. I could feel protected to experience peace. I deserved that, and I would create that.

When I sat with my desires, I realized my creative side was yearning to be acknowledged, my ability to write and draw was being neglected, and these "tools" of mine, which are readily available, could provide the stability I needed.

Self-love may mean different things to you: it could be prioritizing yourself by signing up for that ceramics class you've always wanted to take, or it could be leaning into your spiritual side instead of staying home to watch murder mysteries on repeat.

Self-love is about speaking to and about yourself with love. I believe in "I Am" or "I Trust" statements. "I can show myself the compassion that I show others" or "I trust that healthy relationships will be revealed to me" are examples of statements that give you strength. You know that saying, "fake it till you make it"? It can apply here. If you have a tough time generating self-love, just speaking these sentences can help. They can make you feel that you can handle this someday. Don't focus on self-love coming immediately, because it'll feel foreign when you first begin. But this is one of the main things you can do in your own recovery.

Allow yourself to step away from the situation and focus on your life. Here's a helpful mantra: "I choose myself." Breathe in. Breathe out. Repeat. You can sprinkle in some profanity: "I choose myfuckingself"; "I fucking choose myself." Either would work.

Gentle Heads Up

It's worth mentioning that sometimes acts of self-love could make the addict angrier. You may be accused of making their addiction worse, of not caring about them, or even be called some expletives I shall not name. You may find yourself on the receiving end of their anger when you begin to set healthy boundaries: no longer responding to texts after a certain hour, refraining from loaning money, or ceasing to make excuses for them to your family. It's okay. I promise you are doing nothing wrong. They will adjust just like you had to adjust to their addiction in the beginning. Do not let their harshness stop you from reclaiming your life.

Reflection Time

If you love an addict, it is safe to assume that you have experienced chronic stress. In what ways does chronic stress show up for you? This may be either a physical or mental manifestation, or both.

____

____

____

____

____

____

Do you ever engage in negative self-talk? If so, what or who does it sound like?

____

____

____

____

____

____

How are you able to counteract it?

____

____

____

____

____

____

Take a moment to think about how resilient you are. You can thrive in the worst of conditions. What are some ways that you can support yourself when experiencing symptoms of chronic stress? You don't have to be creative here, just think about what lets you exhale even just a little bit. Keep it simple and fill in the list below:

1. ____________________________________

____

2. ____________________________________

____

3. ____________________________________

____

4. ____________________________________

____

5. ____________________________________

____

How do you define self-love?

____

____

____

____

____

What does this look like for you?

____

____

____

____

____

How can you build this into your daily life?

____

____

____

____

____

____

Take a moment to write down a reminder that you are doing nothing wrong when practicing self-love.

____

____

____

____

____

____

Trace the statement below:

I WILL PRACTICE SELF-LOVE.

CHAPTER SEVEN
Listen to Rafiki

The Lion King was released in 1994; I was 10 years old then. To say I loved *The Lion King* would be an understatement. I got *The Lion King* book and a cassette tape of the soundtrack and would play it on repeat in my Jackson Pollock-inspired room. Yes, my mom let me splatter paint my room, much like Jackson Pollock's paintings (love you, mom). Before I flipped the tape to Side B, they would play the section with Rafiki. Rafiki is a kindred spirit, a shaman, a spirit guide, and I love him. I adore his laugh, his little drawing of Simba when he realizes he's still alive, and especially his stick.

Rafiki feels like an old soul I should listen to. I loved the part where he hits Simba over the head with his stick. In response to Simba's question about why he was hit, Rafiki quickly says that it doesn't matter; it's in the past! As Simba rubs his head, he mutters that the past can still hurt. Rafiki sweetly agrees but adds that one can either run from the past or learn from it. I loved how Simba dodged Rafiki's next attempt, grabbed Rafiki's stick, and threw it, all while Rafiki laughed, enjoying Simba's reaction.

Looking back, Rafiki's message was like a foreshadowing. I would be hit by that stick a couple of times, but I'd take that fucking stick and fling it as far as I could (much like the toaster). I carried the message with me and faced the fact that learning from the past would require vulnerability, accountability, and evolution. No, I hadn't experienced the same trauma as Simba, but I was a changed person, and we both preferred isolating ourselves over facing the hard truths in our lives. While I'd much rather eat bugs and lay around with Timon and Pumbaa, it was not what our journeys were meant for.

Truth Hurts But Evolve Anyways

The truth does fucking hurt; the past does fucking hurt. It wrecks you that your loved one may never see the light, and you will have to witness it. Of course, because of your love for them, you might not want to do what's necessary. However, the love you have for yourself must be even stronger. It just does.

This may require you to leave. This may require you to set boundaries that make you uncomfortable. This may require you to limit their time with your children. This may require you to retrieve your own car. This may require you to grow and evolve as a person. Regardless of whatever difficult position you have been put in, remember that transformation is not convenient, and inconvenience is often required for genuine change.

At one point, I was so pissed at my husband because I didn't want to get back into therapy. I resented him because I thought, "I'm only struggling because of him; it's *his* fault." I was angry that his issues seemingly forced me to look at my choices, ultimately making me evolve. Honestly, I wasn't the one who realized this; it was Kate, the wise psychologist friend I mentioned earlier. She said, "It sounds like you are *really* angry that he's making you evolve." "Yes, Kate, FINE, you are right! But I don't have to be happy about it," I replied.

The Truth Behind the Blame Game

By saying, *"it's all your fault!"* I said he controlled the situation and took *my* control away from me. I had every right to feel this way because his actions deeply hurt me and impacted my life. However, making an all-encompassing statement like *"it's all your fault!"* felt self-serving and self-indulgent. It distracted me from my opportunities for personal growth, providing me with an excuse not to pursue them.

I found myself in a blame spiral. This gave rise to intense feelings of sadness and rage. I would often visualize a witch with a big wart on her nose, leaning over her boiling pot. As she watched my reflection in her bubbles, her eyes widened and she would whisper, "yesss, yesss" when the bubbles grew larger. Whenever I spoke, negativity poured out, which I despised. However, blaming him had become a habit, something familiar. It was like a muscle I exercised daily until it grew massive. This became a steady, predictable pattern. I settled into that pattern for a while, even though it harmed me.

I later realized that lounging in my blame cloud, was actually a form of experiential avoidance which, in the end, actually exacerbated my problems. From an ACT perspective, experiential avoidance occurs when a person continually avoids certain feelings, thoughts, or memories that will cause distress. If I had to change my life and stop blaming my husband, I knew I'd likely have to separate, and this caused a stabbing pain in my chest. Separating would force me to face my fears around being alone, financial insecurity, and single parenting, just to name a few. I did not want to think about it or feel even a moment of that pain, but deep down, I knew that my Schwarzenegger muscle of blame needed to atrophy; it was inevitable.

Experiential avoidance stuck around so long that it became a mainstay in my life, leading to cognitive fusion. Cognitive fusion occurred because I became so tightly attached to my thoughts that the thoughts became my reality – we are the stories we tell ourselves. I would label and limit myself with the narrative I created in my mind around his addiction in connection to me. For example, I'd think, "I can't go to sleep until he's home safe," or "I am a failure because I can't get him to get help," or "If people know about his addiction, they'll judge me as a wife and therapist." These statements were harsh and so fucked up to say to myself, but they were so easy to fall into. Once I repeated them repeatedly; I began to believe them. Once I believed them, they became "rules" in my life. These "rules" kept me from seeing my options.

Leaning into my ACT training, I helped challenge these "rules" I created. I'm not a fan of authority. So why was I dictating my life and binding myself to these stupid rules? I had to challenge these thoughts and distance myself from these harmful rules. While it felt like pulling a sticky, old Band-Aid from an infected wound, I began to do it slowly, with compassion, and action. If I stayed up late until he got home, it only made me more tired the next day and less present for my son, which inevitably impacted my negative self-view.

So instead, I went to bed when I was exhausted. I woke up the following day, and the world hadn't blown up. When I felt like a failure because he wouldn't start treatment, I'd write down a list of things I had accomplished and the statement: "I am only responsible for myself." When I felt the urge to make excuses for him, I'd go to an Al-Anon meeting or call a friend. They reminded me that his choices are not a reflection on me, and I do not have to hide or clean up his mess. When I was in a relatively healthy state of mind, I'd try to expand my perspective, and go much deeper, like Rafiki, seeking wisdom in deeper truths.

All In The Way You Frame It

I'm going to get all spiritual on you: this is just my creative way of thinking and viewing life, so bear with me. The structure could be clearer: "Suppose Earth is a school where we are taught that the perceived "bad" things happening to us are not because of "bad luck" or "chance"," they have instead been given to us as gifts for our evolution. When I begin to go down a negative spiral, I sit back and think, *"What am I being asked to learn from this experience?"* Maybe I'm being asked to learn self-love, to demonstrate more compassion, or to accept help from others and acknowledge when I cannot handle things on my own. When it comes to life or the afterlife, I often say, "All I know is that I don't know." None of us really knows what is going on in this life, galaxy, and beyond; however, as humans, we are often internally driven to find meaning, which is probably why I view things this way (But I do find it helpful; that's why I'm sharing it!). The next time you feel that the school of life is forcing a lesson down your throat, ask yourself, *"What am I missing? What do I need to learn?"* Ask these questions gently and lovingly. It's okay that you may not understand, but honestly, I don't even know why I'm surrounded by addiction. If I had my way, I wouldn't, but there is something that led me here, and because of that, I will lean into my experience and grow.

I want to acknowledge how much I've grown. I began focusing on my life. I started writing and drawing, instead of going straight from sessions to the nighttime routine with my son. I even hired a babysitter so I could take a yoga class. In the past, I would have felt immense guilt if I didn't spend every waking moment with him. But to be the best mom and overall person, I had to take care of myself first. What was I modeling to him anyway? To run yourself ragged? I owe it to both him and myself to set a better example.

Reflection Time

Have you ever been frustrated, dumbfounded, angry, or confused as to why you were going through this experience with the addict?

____

____

____

____

____

What do you believe about why certain experiences happen in your life?

____

____

____

____

____

Can you reframe your thoughts to look at this as an opportunity to evolve?

____

____

____

____

____

How can you begin to put the focus back on your life and stop assigning fault?

____

____

____

____

____

Can you give yourself permission to release any negative feelings around prioritizing yourself?

____

____

____

____

____

____

Repeat after me: THIS HURTS BUT EVOLVE ANYWAYS

Remember:

"These are the days that must happen to you." – Walt Whitman

CHAPTER EIGHT
You Contain Multitudes

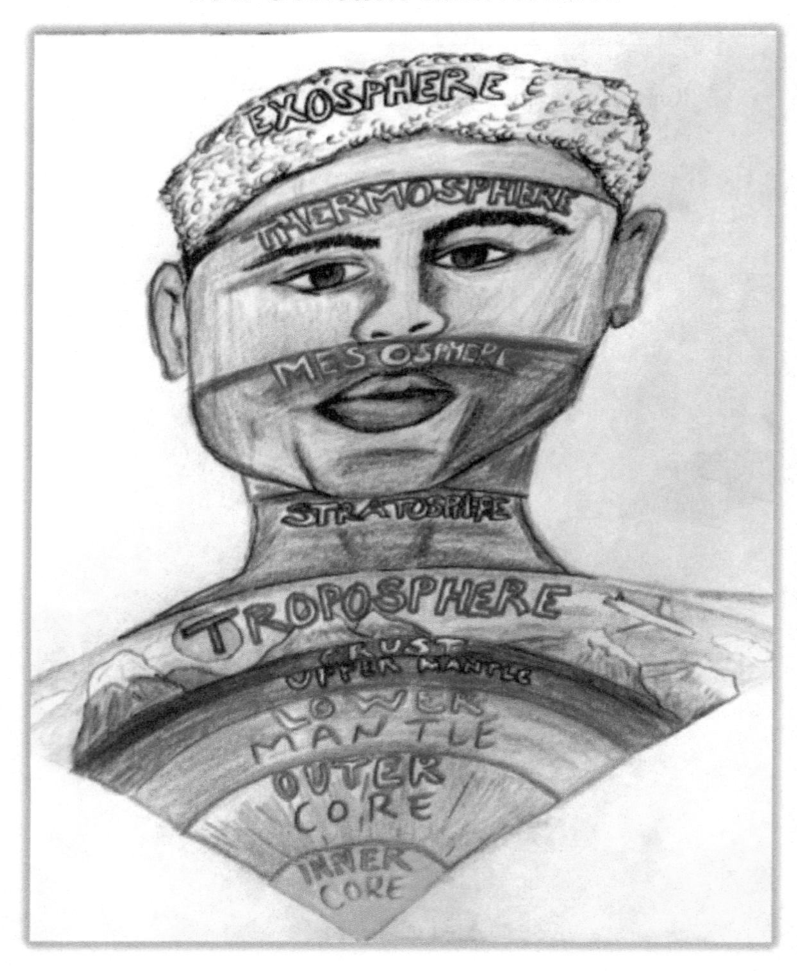

As you've probably come to realize, I've been to hell and back — and back again. Through this thick, disgusting, sticky mud, I've learned that what you resist persists; so it's best to just surrender. As both a licensed therapist and a human being dealing with the impacts of addiction, I understand that when you're in the midst of it — right in the heart of that tunnel — you can lose yourself. It's dim, disorienting, and, frankly, smells like shit. I've discovered that reclaiming ownership over your life is the best way to begin your journey through that tunnel to the other side — though you might still find remnants of hard, dry mud clinging to your skin.

After journeying through this pain alongside me, I urge you, my dear readers, to prioritize self-care. Yes, you deserve it, and I'd venture to guess that you need it. See, you are more than you probably give yourself credit for. To put this more eloquently, I will quote the great Walt Whitman, *"I am large. I contain multitudes."* Let me explain. When loving an addict, the poem that gives me the most comfort and understanding is *Songs of Myself, 51*, by Walt Whitman. He wrote:

> *The past and present wilt—I have fill'd them, emptied them.*
> *And proceed to fill my next fold of the future.*
> *Listener up there! what have you to confide to me?*
> *Look in my face while I snuff the sidle of evening,*
> *(Talk honestly, no one else hears you, and I stay only a minute longer.)*
> *Do I contradict myself?*
> *Very well then, I contradict myself,*

(I am large, I contain multitudes.)
I concentrate toward them that are nigh,
I wait on the door-slab.
Who has done his day's work? who will soonest be through with his supper?
Who wishes to walk with me?
Will you speak before I am gone? will you prove already too late?

Whenever I approach "The Overwhelm," I read this beautiful piece of early American poetry and feel seen. The irony, earnestness, cagey humor, and contradictions in this work make me feel safe. I often think that if Whitman, Ashcroft, and Rafiki were contemporaries, they'd be best buds. I can hear Whitman speak to me from beyond the grave, offering wise words to those who love an addict. Of course, many view Whitman as addressing someone or something greater than himself. Some interpret this as God, while others think he's addressing the reader. Nevertheless, I believe he's communicating with an entity he trusts with his profoundest truths.

This is what I hear and feel:

1. Life is crazy fast. Don't hold back.
2. Be honest. Be honest with yourself and with others. There is no life in living in denial, fear, or the past.
3. Don't give too many fucks because life is over in a blink of an eye.
4. Be present. Take advantage of this moment.
5. Don't sell yourself short. You are not one thing; you are many things. You are ever-evolving.

You are Vast

I Am Large. I Contain Multitudes." This simple statement is for you, dear readers, because you contain multitudes. You are not just this one experience. While addiction is all-consuming and complex, you are also complex; therefore, this is not your only identity or journey in life. You are full of beautiful parts that need to be seen. You are vast. If you zoom out and look at your life from a macro perspective, as if you were sitting on the Moon observing yourself as Earth, you will see all your layers, all the way to the exosphere, and the storms you have weathered, from earthquakes to avalanches. If you look inside yourself, past the flesh and bones, you will find the layers of your being, your essence, what makes you… you.

While we can obtain samples of the Earth's mantle for direct measurement, no samples of the Earth's core are accessible. We still know it exists, even though we cannot physically examine it. Much like the Earth, there is a non-physical core inside you that we know is powerful, even though we cannot look at it under a microscope. This part of you is sacred, one you should protect, and protection can come by reframing how you view your experiences.

You can look at your experience of loving an addict as the massive asteroid predicted to take the Earth down. Or you can see it as the break in the pipe that flooded your basement, slightly warping your hardwood floor. Instead of stepping into the water to use a Shop-Vac (yes, Chelsie and I did this without electrocuting ourselves to death), you can call in an expert. They can help rebuild those floors and take over where you lack expertise. You don't have to be completely overwhelmed by the situation; acknowledging your limits and understanding when something is beyond your capability is key. It can be a minor blip on the radar, not the life destroyer you thought it would be.

Since you contain multitudes, you will not stay the same, because you were never supposed to. I hope you understand that while loving an addict is tragic and messy, it is not for you to fix. Through acceptance and focus on yourself, things can and will improve. This is not merely toxic positivity. It will get better – not "all better," but indeed, better. However, how much "better" it becomes is up to you. It's a given that life will throw some shitty challenges your way, but remember, you are in control of your response. You may surprise yourself with your ability to handle even the worst circumstances.

While I can't, and would never, promise a "fairytale ending" with "closed loops" and "hemmed edges" (because those do not exist), I can promise that there is freedom in finding yourself again and embracing the "bittersweet." It is hard and chaotic, and at times the path to freeing yourself from the clutches of addiction will feel too much to bear—but know that you are not alone and that you are all you need. *Do I contradict myself?* Very well then, I contradict myself :)

ACKNOWLEDGMENTS

This book would not be in existence without Timothy Gordon, aka "The Zen Social Worker." There are few people in this world who will come along and truly see you, flaws and all, and know that you are great, even before you do, and invite you to rise to that greatness. This is what Tim did for me. I am forever grateful to you.

Leslie: Nothing I write here will properly express my gratitude to you. You have been one of my greatest teachers. Thank you for allowing me to include your story as I see it. You are fucking brave. I love you.

Mom and Dad: This is a reminder that you are great parents :) You are two vibrant lights that, together, create a spotlight leading me home. Thank you for bringing me into this world, and for loving me with all your heart. I love you both immensely.

T: Thank you for creating the beautiful person that is our boy. Thank you for the lessons that created a welcomed detour: this book. I love you, but I still *hate* your addiction :)

Jules Micah: You will read this one day, and while this worries me sometimes, I know that bringing the truth into the light is always the best way to go. I hope you always do this for yourself. I love you.

Keagan and Bella: I am so lucky to have watched both of you grow from birth into the creative geniuses that you are. I love you both so much.

Chelsie: You are my partner in crime and my bestie for life. I couldn't have survived that summer without you. Thank God for Michael Bolton. I love you.

Kate: Thank you for your brilliant mind and for never fearing to speak the truth. You are a gift.

Heather: Thank you for enthusiastically reading every bit of my writing and giving me endless feedback and support. We've already lived this life together. The synchronicities are undeniable, and it all started on that couch in Astoria, watching "The Conversation."

Lisa: My sister friend, you are a golden/red beam of light that fills up my cup. Thank you for being you.

Yvette: Your words and support helped save me during the depths of my pain. Your encouragement kept me from doubting myself. I am so grateful for you (shout out to Bella and Dave!).

Malaika: Thank you for your vulnerability and guiding me to the support system that I didn't know I needed.

Megan: You are my manifesting partner and hype man. Thank you for helping me step into my greatness. <3

Anya: From the second I shared this book idea with you, you cheered me on. Love you. Xx.

Usher: I can't thank you enough for bringing this book into the world. Thank you for taking a chance on me and believing in this book's healing powers.

Everyone at Library Tales Publishing: Thank you for working on this book and supporting my vision!

I have received encouragement, support, and inspiration from many including but not limited to: Tonya, Kristie, Kolina, Gina, Margarita, Anna, Amelia, Marsha, Livy, the Xinalani ladies, Taylor, Lana, my subscribers, and all my clients, past and present.

Made in the USA
Columbia, SC
20 September 2023